HOLLY CLEGG'S trim&TERRIFIC®

Too Hot in the Kitchen

Secrets to Sizzle At Any Age — 200 Simple and Sassy Recipes

Library of Congress Control Number: 2010907551

ISBN-13   978-0-9815640-1-2

ISBN-10   0-9815640-1-1

Cover and interior book design by TILT (www.tiltthis.com)

Edited by Lee Jackson, LDN, RD

Illustrations by Amy Saidens

Photography edited by Claire Strebeck

Creative consulting by Pamela Clegg Hill

Nutritional Analysis: Tammi Hancock, Hancock Nutrition

Other Books by Holly Clegg:

Holly Clegg's trim&TERRIFIC® Gulf Coast Favorites

The New Holly Clegg trim&TERRIFIC® Cookbook

Holly Clegg's trim&TERRIFIC® Home Entertaining The Easy Way

Holly Clegg's trim&TERRIFIC® Freezer Friendly Meals

Holly Clegg's trim&TERRIFIC® Diabetic Cooking

Eating Well Through Cancer: Easy Recipes & Recommendations Before & After Treatment

To order books, call **1-800-88HOLLY** or visit **www.hollyclegg.com** or **www.thehealthycookingblog.com**

Production and Manufacturing:

Favorite Recipes Press

An imprint of FRP

P.O. Box 305142 Nashville, TN 37230

800-358-0560

Acknowledgments

Darling Divas... Since the focus of this book is women, I am acknowledging the females this time *(spouses you know what you mean to me)*. However, there are a few men in my life that make a difference. My husband, **Mike**, continually supports and encourages me to go after my dreams, there to root me on and there to pick me up; and tolerates all the food I overwhelm him with! As my daughter **Haley** says, we are the best when we are together, an unbeatable team. **My Father** is an inspiration and testimonial to life, and who always one ups me with a standing ovation every time he speaks to a room of kids about not smoking, doing so with his artificial larynx from a bout with larynx cancer! A true hero — so proud of him! **Todd**, my son, working in private equity, gives me the gift of calling me on his daily walk to work, the one time I don't talk about cooking and enjoy my Todd time! **Chad**, my Dallas son takes such good care of my daughter and I think he is the best at whatever he does! **Robert** still out cooks me with gumbos and fish — just not trim and terrific! *My Daughter Divas:* **Courtney**, my recipe for a beautiful person inside and out — a special bond, caring, giving, advising and loving — so very proud of you. **Haley** *(my baby)*, my recipe for life-persistence, adorable, smart and inexhaustible with a contagious smile whether reading my cookbook or cooking, you make it all more fun. **Sana**, my recipe for the best daughter-in-law with determination to succeed, consideration for all, caring for my son and sharing your life with me as a daughter — I am so fortunate when I think of you. *Mama Divas:* **My Mother** has taught me life lessons with values that I know have made me the person I am today — thank you Mother! **Mae Mae**, my in town mom who is there for me from tasting, testing, making that last grocery run, helping me shop, and taking care of Elvis. *Sister Divas:* **Ilene**, my recipe for a sister — you listen and advise, care and share, always there, and even cook... sometimes. **Pam**, my recipe for bonding — we share so much from fun to family, cooking and more cooking, and enjoy time together, rather in a kitchen or at a spa. *Managing Divas:* **Lee**, life without you is unimaginable — you're smart, hang with me from cooking, office work or walking and make my life not so crazy — thank you! *Diva Dog:* **Elvis**, the one I can count on always happy to see me — in my office, kitchen and now in my book.

Cookbook diva dream team...

Thanks to my *Dependable Divas* who run my office: My Satellite Office- **Karen**, who pulls so much weight, Home Office- **Lee**, my right hand and left and, and, and... what is your job description? Corporate Office- **Courtney**, my sounding and advisement board, **Haley and Pam**, run my test kitchens; **Sana**, runs my creative department. *Designer Divas:* **Amy Saidens**, my illustrator who mastered my vision of this book with creativity and precision — creating my ultimate "diva". **TILT**, my design team (not divas but definitely on my team) — calm and calculating every page while I ramble, to give me an incredible design for this book. **Tammi Hancock**, another book and another nutritional analysis — over 10 years with me. **Sheila and FRP**, keep those printing presses rolling! *Dynamite Diva:* Last, but surely not least, a big Texas size thank you to **Edelman Public Relations Firm** in Dallas — Jen and your team for your expertise, time, and commitment for "cooking up" excitement for the book. I had a vision for this book, and all of you made this vision possible!

Diva friends that heat up the kitchen...

Creative Cooks: **Melanie**, cooks up masterpieces, **Jolie-olie**, cooks up memories, **Amy**, cooks like a gem, **Melinda**, my partner in cooking business, **Missy**, cooks with style. *Convenience Cooks:* **Karen**, cooks on the run. **Kaye**, extra cook, **Donna**, triples the recipe. *Pick-up Cooks:* **Anisa**, figures out cooking, **Joyce**, cooks up reservations, **Aunt Garney**, on-the-go cook, **Kim**, coordinates cooking. *Casual Cooks:* **Gracie**, care-taker cook, and my co-eater, **Sherri**, cosmetic cooking, **Gail**, cooking on demand, **Selma**, cooks with finesse, **Leslie**, cooks on the move, **Marty**, camp cooking, **Lila**, long-time cook, **Renate**, my English cook, **Terri**, original hotty in the kitchen. *Constant Cooks:* **Louann**, cooks as much as I do, **Marcia**, the ultimate cook, **Lynell**, my groupie cook, **Mocklers, Cliffords, and Sligars**, my neighborhood cooks. *Comfort Cooks:* **Francine**, best comfort food cook, **Mary**, nails traditional cooking. *Experienced Cooks:* **Melanie**, my advisor cook, **Jill**, my first cooking friend, **Sheila**, cooks page by page.

Cooking Up Business...

I have been fortunate to represent and work with the best people and products who allow me to practice my passion of testing, creating, and work with you: Louisiana yams- Diane Allen & Associates- Al and Diane, Mizkan-Nakano seasoned rice vinegars, Holland House Cooking wines- Teresa and Maruta, Tyson Grilled and Ready Chicken Breasts, Jana and Catherine, Walmart- Great Value products, Emily, American Chemistry Council- Janel and Rachelle. Gerald- ok...my token male who is my partner in the cancer cookbook, my most rewarding endeavor.

Introduction

This cookbook is for women of all ages, with a focus on their demands and their needs. With the same passion and appreciation for good food as in all my trim&TERRIFIC® cookbooks, my newest creation adds a fun, whimsical and entertaining approach to healthier recipes designed for busy women.

Several years ago my friend, Terri, kept fanning herself and said, "You need to write a book for women having hot flashes—maybe all cold recipes." That is where my vision for *Too Hot in the Kitchen* began, and I expanded the idea to encompass all women as they experience and embrace the many stages of life.

Eating healthier can easily be a way of life; therefore, my first chapter, "Foods To Improve", gives an overview of what healthy foods to include in your daily diet. And, when it's hot outside or those hot flashes hit, "Lovin' No Oven" features only cold recipes. Romance is in the air with "Food for the Mood" and whether you are newly married or in the empty nest stage, "Table for Two" will help you cook for a pair. "Quickies" of course, contains all super fast recipes. Another fun facet to this book is coffee pairing. Just as wine has its place with food, so does coffee. You can become a Coffee Connoisseur and learn that coffee compliments different foods by looking for the coffee cup next to the recipe.

One of my favorite chapters, "Diva Dermatology", includes facials made with everyday food. To help me test the recipes, I invited my friends over *(without makeup!)* for our very own diva party. Did you know you can glow simply from an Avocado mask?

I have been deemed "the queen of quick" as I believe in time-friendly, pantry-friendly, and user-friendly recipes, allowing you to prepare a healthier meal on those hectic days. With my new book, *Too Hot in the Kitchen*, you will have the recipes to sizzle through every stage of your life.

Each recipe includes the nutritional analysis and the diabetic exchange. The analysis is based on the larger serving. The nutritional analysis does not include any salt or pepper *(since it is listed to taste)* or any ingredient with "optional" after it.

The recipes in this book also feature icons to help you know which are dishes are **Freezer-Friendly** and which are **Vegetarian.**

Freezer-friendly recipes that you can make ahead

Vegetarian recipes

And what Diva book would be complete without some spicy advice? Look for these throughout the book for serving suggestions and cooking tidbits.

Coffee & Food Pairing

COFFEE FOR EVERY OCCASION

You've heard of pairing certain wines with different foods, well the same goes with coffee. When pairing coffee with food, you want to make sure that the coffee flavor complements rather than overpowers the food. Coffee comes from all around the world and different regions are known for their different types of coffee. However, coffee is very personal so have fun experimenting to find your favorite coffee pairings. You can easily become your own Coffee Connoisseur with these simple guidelines:

» *Mild foods are best with mild coffees, while rich foods pair best with intense coffees.*

» *Those in the south/southwest enjoy more highly seasoned food, so a darker bolder roast coffee is preferred. In parts of the country where food is not seasoned as much, a milder roast coffee is used.*

» *When it comes to dessert, just remember, the richer the dessert, the darker the roast you can serve to go with it.*

» *Coffee scoop= 2 tablespoons coffee to use with 6 ounces water*

Think about this: chocolate, coffee, and men... *some things are better rich!*

MEDIUM-LIGHT ROASTS

HAWAIIAN KONA a spicy rich aromatic lighter coffee with a bit of cinnamon and clove. **Foods:** cookies (oatmeal), coffee cakes, pancakes, milk chocolate, snacks, fruit desserts, seafood, poultry.

MEXICAN a smooth coffee with a delicate snap of hazelnut. **Foods:** brunch, goes with muffins, eggs, and lighter fares, nuts, milk chocolate, loaf cakes and cream pies, poultry, seafood.

MEDIUM ROASTS

COLUMBIAN a full rich coffee with sweet caramel flavor. **Foods:** carrot cake, cheesecake, Tiramisu, creamy desserts, milk or white chocolate, quick breads with nuts (banana), mild simple breakfast food.

ETHIOPIAN a rich coffee with fruity tones, hints of wine, lemon, cinnamon and blueberry. **Foods:** Chinese or Asian, ginger, Mediterranean, quick breads, savory, buttery, salty dishes, milk chocolate.

JAVA a coffee with a spicy aroma with an exotic, smooth flavor. **Foods:** savory brunch foods like omelets, cheeses, mushrooms and basil.

MEDIUM-DARK ROASTS

COSTA RICAN a rich full-bodied fragrant coffee with smooth, delicate, yet smoky flavor. **Foods:** lightly flavored baked items, fruit muffins, white chocolate, caramel, milk chocolate, citrus fruit, cinnamon rolls, desserts, eggs/bacon-brunch, seafood.

BRAZILIAN a smooth and subtle natural and chocolate flavor with nutty tones. **Foods:** chocolate desserts, dark chocolate, nuts, mild flavored breakfast foods.

GUATEMALAN a lively aroma with a chocolatey, subtle, smoky flavor.
Foods: chocolate cake, brownies, cheesecake, afternoon coffee, caramel desserts, fruit and cheese, roasted meats.

KENYAN an intensely fragrant floral coffee with wine, chocolate and berry undertones. **Foods:** carrot cake, creamy desserts like tiramisu or trifle, fruit pies, berry desserts, Indian or Thai food, orange-flavor, or stewed meats.

DARK ROASTS

SUMATRAN a complex, exotic and deeply aromatic coffee. **Foods:** savory foods, meat and potato meal, tomato sauces, lamb, cheesy dishes, savory brunch foods, cinnamon flavors, Thai with peanut butter, rich cheesecake, rich, heavy desserts, rich chocolate desserts, chocolate truffle, pecan pie.

FRENCH ROAST either love or hate this light-bodied intense smoky extra bold coffee. **Foods:** rich deep dark chocolate desserts, nutty desserts, mousse, roasted veggies,caramelized sugar desserts, grilled meats/fish, smoked meats/cheeses, Cajun/Creole.

ITALIAN ROAST a bold medium-bodied coffee with a slightly sweet aroma
Foods: rich chocolate and caramelized sugar sweets.

FLAVORED COFFEE

Dessert coffee with a variety of flavors available such as French vanilla, hazelnut, southern pecan, chocolate, caramel, cinnamon offers a satisfying, smooth and slightly sweet aroma. **Foods:** biscotti, butter cookies, coffeecake.

ESPRESSO

A very bold, full-bodied coffee with a spicy aroma and dense caramel flavor. **Foods:** perfect foundation for a latte or cappuccino, dark rich chocolate, truffle, caramel, spices and nuts.

Berry Good Oatmeal Cookie Cake

Foods to Improve

From the inside out, foods add pleasure to our day and health to our life. Although I do not believe in ruling out certain foods while only eating others, there are a certain few that you should make sure to include regularly for optimum health and disease prevention. Focus on what to eat instead of what not to eat! And guess what? Don't think of eating these foods as a chore as some of them are my very favorite foods anyway! **Avocados, berries, spices** and **sweet potatoes** – you surely can eat well while eating deliciously.

AVOCADO

Did you know buttery green avocados are considered a fruit--rich in heart-healthy monounsaturated (good) fat and one of the most nutrient-dense foods.

- Avocados are high in fiber and, ounce for ounce; top the charts among all fruits for folate, potassium, vitamin E, and magnesium.
- Rich in magnesium which is an essential nutrient for healthy bones.
- Avocados boost the same good health effects as olive oil.

BEANS

Baked beans, black beans, lima beans, kidney beans, white, red, pinto, Lima, split, garbanzo, and lentils just might be magical – as the children's rhyme goes. The humble bean is inexpensive and vastly versatile while also a good source of protein, fiber, vitamins, and antioxidants.

- By eating beans often you can reduce your risk of heart disease, stroke and, some types of cancer.
- Beans are loaded with soluble fiber, which fill you up, helping to control weight.

BERRIES

Whether you choose strawberries, blueberries, raspberries, cranberries, or blackberries, these little jewels are packed with fiber and antioxidants that help slow the aging process from the inside out.

- From memory protection, reduced risk of cancers, and decreased infections, make sure you eat berries daily to benefit from all they have to offer.
- Frozen do the trick as well as fresh, and can be in the freezer year-round.
- Berries deliver delicious taste and nutrition with few calories.

CRUCIFEROUS VEGETABLES

Members of the cruciferous vegetable family include broccoli, cauliflower, cabbage, Brussels sprouts, kale, bok choy and, collard greens.

- Loaded with fiber, which is important for reducing the risk for certain cancers, as well as helping the body maintain a healthy weight.
- Did you know broccoli has as much calcium as a glass of milk and more vitamin C than an orange and is a powerful brain protector.

DAIRY

Dairy products are good sources of protein, vitamin D, potassium, and especially calcium, which is very important for women of all ages.

- You don't have to just drink your milk; foods such as low-fat yogurt, cheese and cottage cheese are great for you too!

- Calcium is absorbed best from foods rather than supplements- make sure to get at least three servings of calcium-rich foods every day.

- Dairy is important for building strong teeth and bones, but may also help reduce your risk of high blood pressure, kidney stones, heart disease, colon cancer, as well as helping in weight management.

FISH

Certain fish rich in the essential fatty acid, omega-3 fatty acid, include salmon, tuna, trout, and sardines. Try to eat these heart healthy fish twice a week.

- Fish is an excellent source of high-quality lean protein while also providing tons of nutritional benefits without a lot of calories.

- Eating foods high in omega-3 fatty acids regularly is important for brain health, decreasing risk of Alzheimer's disease, as well as reducing the risk of heart disease.

- Helping to reduce blood clots and blood pressure, lowering cholesterol levels, cancer risk, and reducing the risk of depression are other fantastic benefits of omega-3 fatty acids.

NUTS

Nuts tend to be higher in fat and calories so don't go "nuts" eating too many, however they do contain a host of health benefits making them worthy of being included in your meals and snacks.

- The fat in nuts is mostly those good-for-you unsaturated fats, helping to prevent heart disease, lower cholesterol, and promote brain health.

- Nuts provide fiber, protein, potassium, magnesium, omega-3 fatty acids and vitamins E and B6 – a great snack to have on hand to keep blood sugar and energy levels stable.

- Did you know that pecans contain the highest amount of antioxidants than any other nut?

SOY

This plant-based protein contains as much complete protein as meat but much lower in fat – making it an excellent alternative in meatless meals.

- Soy is found in products like tofu, soymilk, and edamame – and help to prevent heart disease by lowering cholesterol.
- Fresh, canned, dried, or frozen – soybeans, such as edamame can easily be thrown into many meals – just think of them as the new green pea!

SPICE UP YOUR LIFE:

You have the keys to health right in your pantry – spices!

- **Cinnamon** may be an important spice in helping to control blood sugar levels in diabetics, as well as increase the good cholesterol and lower the bad cholesterol levels. Cinnamon is also a great source of antioxidants.
- **Garlic** has so many healthy benefits due to its high antioxidant content, such as boosting your immune system, helping to reduce blood pressure as well as reducing the risk for certain cancers.
- **Ginger** has been used for centuries because of its medicinal properties. Protecting against cancer, and boosting your immune system, ginger has long been a remedy for nausea, providing a safe option for expecting mothers with morning sickness.
- **Oregano** is found to be a major component in Italian dishes and has the highest content of antioxidants, important for disease prevention. Fresh or dried, it may also have antibacterial properties.
- **Red Peppers**, from paprika to chili powder, turn up the heat as the hotter the pepper, the more antioxidants they contain. Red pepper may also help control appetite.

SPINACH

You know spinach must be good for you because of its rich color: Proof that this leafy green contains many vitamins, minerals and antioxidants.

- Just 1/2 cup of cooked spinach has 25% of daily folate needs which is especially important for expecting moms – helping prevent a type of birth defect in unborn babies.
- Try eating spinach regularly to help with heart health as well as eye health.

SWEET POTATOES

Sweet potatoes or yams, as they are called in Louisiana, are so nutrient-rich while being low in fat and sodium.

- Sweet potatoes contain 1/3 the daily amount of vitamin C and twice the recommended daily allowance of vitamin A.
- Their luscious bright orange color is due to their high amount of the nutrient, beta-carotene – which may help reduce the risk of certain cancers.

TOMATOES

The tomato is wonderfully versatile in many favorite recipes – and what is better than a ripe juicy red tomato!

- Tomatoes are high in vitamin C and the antioxidant lycopene.
- Lycopene is not produced in the body so it must be eaten in lycopene-rich foods but is important for disease-fighting especially some cancers.

WATER

Did you know that the average person loses about 2 1/2 quarts of water each day – and more if the weather is hot and humid? It is important to hydrate yourself throughout the day to replace the loss of water.

- Every cell in your body needs water, in fact, three-fourths of your brain is made of water so drink up to stay sharp!
- Staying well hydrated nourishes your skin, as well as helps flush your body, especially the kidneys, of toxins.
- You've heard it before – aim to drink 6-8 glasses per day.
- Water comes from the food you eat too, especially fruits and vegetables, as if we need another reason to eat plenty of them!

WHOLE GRAINS

Brown rice, wild rice, oatmeal, whole wheat flour, and bulgur – all are various whole grains that provide ample health benefits so try to get the recommended at least 3 servings per day.

- Whole grains are high in fiber, which is important for digestive health, preventing certain diseases and maintaining glucose control – especially for diabetics.

- Make sure you check the ingredient lists on food labels for the word "whole" to appear as the first ingredient listed.

Italian Vegetable Soup

Eat With Color

We all know we should eat healthy, but have you ever wondered where to begin? Make it simple and just remember to eat with color. Green, yellow, red, orange, and purple – the color in fruits and vegetables represents a variety of important nutrients your body needs. A colorful plate ensures you will be eating a wide range of important vitamins and minerals, fiber, and antioxidants for optimum health and energy. They also help to reduce the risk of cancer and disease, while also minimizing the effect of aging. And the brighter the better, as fruits and vegetables richer in color contain more fighting power.

BLUE/PURPLE: *blackberries, blueberries, plums, grapes, raisins, and eggplant – have anti-aging benefits.*

GREEN: *green apples, honeydew melon, kiwi, lime, pears, avocado, asparagus, artichokes, broccoli, kale, collard greens, green peppers, green beans, spinach, zucchini, and green cabbage – helps keep vision sharp and bones and teeth strong; while also helping prevent cancer.*

YELLOW/ORANGE: *apricots, cantaloupe, grapefruit, mango, papaya, peaches, oranges, pineapple, lemons, yellow peppers, pumpkin, sweet potatoes, butternut squash, and carrots – maintains a strong immune system, helps keep vision sharp, and lower your risk of heart disease and cancer.*

RED: *red berries, watermelon, red apples, red peppers, pomegranates, beets, red cabbage, and tomatoes – helps reduce the risk of heart disease and some cancers, while helping to boost your memory.*

WHITE/BROWN: *bananas, dates, cauliflower, garlic, onion, mushrooms, ginger, potatoes, and turnips – helps reduce the risk of heart disease and some cancers.*

BLACK: *CHOCOLATE! I am very happy to say that chocolate contains nutritious antioxidants!*

Diet Dermatology

Lotions and potions can only get you so far in your beauty regime. If you really want radiant beauty, guess where you can find it? Your kitchen! The best skincare secrets come from what you eat so you can improve from the inside out. Good nutrition is important to nourish and protect your skin, as well as minimize the damaging effects of the sun, smog and other stresses life brings us. The best defense is a diet full of antioxidants, vitamins, minerals and lots and lots of water. So it really must be true….you are what you eat!

ANTI-AGING

Nuts, such as almonds, have anti-aging properties which contain vitamin E (an ingredient in anti-wrinkle creams). They also contain high amounts of fatty acids (which help keep skin plump and supple), as well as the antioxidant selenium. (If allergic- wheat germ contains vitamin E too). Walnuts contain fatty acid to calm redness. Pecans are high in antioxidants.

BANISH WRINKLES

Vitamin C is vital for production and formation of collagen, helping to smooth what's on top and prevent wrinkles. A small kiwi contains more than 100 % of recommended daily intake of vitamin C - a real wrinkle-buster! Other great sources of vitamin C are strawberries, oranges, mango, honeydew and papaya.

BOOST MOISTURE

Water, the best skin reviver – can plump skin and make wrinkles less obvious. Drink lots of water (8 glasses daily) as water flushes out toxins, keeps your skin hydrated, rosy and supple.

BRIGHTEN YOUR COMPLEXION

Whole grains like oatmeal are rich in B vitamins, helping to maintain normal skin functions- keeping skin bright, moist, and smooth.

CLEAR SKIN AND ATTACK ACNE

Calcium-rich foods like skim milk, low-fat cheese and yogurt can help keep your skin clear and pimple-free. Foods high in vitamin A, such as broccoli, play a role in healing acne. Dark leafy greens such as spinach and kale, are full of zinc, which has been shown to help clear up skin. Also, zinc helps break down damaged collagen, making room for new collagen to form.

DARK, PUFFY EYES

Up intake of vitamin C and iron; together they are a great way to attack dark under-eye circles!

DEFEAT DRYNESS

Fat is key to a soft complexion, and if you have persistent dry skin you may not be eating enough healthy fats. Olive oil is an extremely healthy fat that helps skin to recover and regenerate new skin cells.

FIGHT FINE LINES

Berries are packed with powerful antioxidants, especially blueberries – a handful of strawberries has all the antioxidant vitamin C your body requires in a day to reconstruct skin's collagen.

FRESH COMPLEXION

Orange, leafy green, and red fruits and veggies such as squash, sweet potatoes, and spinach – are all full of beta-carotene/vitamin A which regulates cell production and turnover so skin's surface is smooth.

HYDRATE AND NOURISH SKIN

Fish high in omega-3 fatty acids, such as salmon, mackerel, bass, and trout calms inflammation, battles free radicals and help smooth fine lines.

SHINY HAIR

Foods rich in vitamin B (eggs, milk, green veggies, and poultry) are fantastic for making dull hair shinier. Minerals found in raw oats, cucumber skin, onions, and bean sprouts help keep hair elastic, shiny, and healthy.

SKIN ELASTICITY

Antioxidants such as vitamins A, C, and E are important for discouraging wrinkles by reducing deep collagen damage. Broccoli has some of the highest level of anti-oxidants, vitamins A and C than any other food. Cantaloupe and red bell peppers also contain high amounts of vitamin A, C, and E, skin super foods!

SOOTHE SUNBURN

Turns out the sweet treats, peaches and blueberries; contain tons of vitamin E — known for easing redness and swelling associated with sunburns. Watermelon is rich in lycopene, providing 33% more protection against sunburn than other fruits.

STRENGTHEN NAILS

Eat protein which helps keep nails strong and moisturized. Protein is what builds up keratin, the substance nails are made up of.

YOUTHFUL GLOW

Fortified cereal, lean meat, pork, poultry, oysters all contain zinc which contributes to cell production and natural cell sloughing keeping dullness away. The iron in these foods is needed by red blood cells to carry oxygen giving your skin a healthy glow.

Strawberry and Mixed Green Salad with Spiced Walnuts

Lovin' No Oven

I don't have hot flashes, *I have short private vacations in the tropics*

Tomato Brushetta

Summer sensation! Nothing beats fresh tomatoes, fresh basil and Kalamatas (from olive bar) for this top-notch refreshing pick-up.

Makes 16 servings (bread with about 2 tablespoons topping)

1 loaf French bread

Garlic cloves or minced garlic

1 1/2 cups finely chopped tomatoes
   (about 1 1/2 pounds, seeded)

1/4 cup chopped Kalamata olives

1/4 cup chopped onion

2 teaspoons olive oil

1 teaspoon balsamic vinegar

5-6 fresh basil leaves, chopped or
   1 teaspoon dried basil leaves

1. Preheat oven 450°F. Slice French bread into thin slices and bake about 10 minutes or until crispy. Remove from oven and rub garlic clove across top.

2. In bowl, combine all remaining ingredients. When ready to serve, top toasted bread.

Spicy Advice

To seed tomatoes: cut tomato in half from side to side and gently squeeze tomato to watch seeds easily pop out.

Tomato Brushetta

Avocado Dip

Edamame adds crunch and sneaks in a nutritional boost combined with powerful flavors into one mouthful of avocado bliss.

Makes 8 (1/4-cup) servings

1 large avocado, (about 2/3 cup mashed)

1 1/2 cups shelled edamame, thawed

3 tablespoons lime juice

1 tablespoon jarred jalapenos

1/2 teaspoon minced garlic

1/2 cup salsa

1/4 cup nonfat sour cream

Salt and pepper to taste

1. In food processor, combine all ingredients, mixing until smooth. Serve immediately.

Nutritional information per serving:
Calories 103
Calories from fat 50%
Fat 6g
Saturated Fat 1g
Cholesterol 1mg
Sodium 93mg
Carbohydrate 8g
Dietary Fiber 4g
Sugars 2g
Protein 5g
Dietary Exchanges:
1/2 starch. 1/2 very lean meat, 1 fat

Guacamole Goes Mediterranean

As an avocado and feta addict, this dip definitely satisfied my cravings.

Makes 5 (1/4 cup) servings

1 cup chopped avocado, (1-2 avocados)

1/4 cup finely chopped red onion

1 teaspoon minced garlic

2 tablespoons finely chopped parsley

1/2 teaspoon dried oregano leaves

1 teaspoon olive oil

1 tablespoon seasoned rice vinegar (basil and oregano flavored)

1/4 cup crumbled reduced-fat feta cheese

1. In bowl, gently stir together avocado, onion, and garlic. Mix in parsley and oregano.

2. Gently stir in olive oil, vinegar and feta. Refrigerate or serve.

Nutritional information per serving:
Calories 123
Calories from fat 72%
Fat 11g
Saturated Fat 2g
Cholesterol 3mg
Sodium 105mg
Carbohydrate 7g
Dietary Fiber 4g
Sugars 1g
Protein 3g
Dietary Exchanges:
1/2 starch, 2 fat

Super Salsa

Nutritional information per serving:
Calories 47
Calories from fat 36%
Fat 2g
Saturated Fat 0g
Cholesterol 0mg
Sodium 151mg
Carbohydrate 7g
Dietary Fiber 2g
Sugars 2g
Protein 1g
Dietary Exchanges:
1 vegetable, 1/2 fat

Open a few cans combined with fresh ingredients for a simple and super snazzy salsa. You can make homemade tortilla chips or pick up a bag.

Makes 16 (1/4 cup) servings

1 (28-ounce) can chopped tomatoes, drained

1 (11-ounce) can Southwestern corn, drained

1 avocado, chopped

1/3 cup chopped green onions

1/2 teaspoon minced garlic

2 tablespoons finely chopped jarred jalapenos

2 tablespoons lime juice

1/4 cup chopped fresh cilantro, optional

Tortilla Chips (recipe follows)

1. In bowl, combine all ingredients. Serve with homemade Tortilla Chips (see recipe below).

Nutritional information per serving:
Calories 73
Calories from fat 0%
Fat 2g
Saturated Fat 0g
Cholesterol 0mg
Sodium 171mg
Carbohydrate 20g
Dietary Fiber 2g
Sugars 0g
Protein 3g
Dietary Exchanges:
1 1/2 starch

Tortilla Chips

Makes great snack. For variation, sprinkle with your favorite seasonings.

Makes 16 (1 tortilla) servings

16 (6-8-inch) whole wheat or white flour tortillas

Water

Preheat oven 425°F. Coat baking sheet with nonstick cooking spray.

Brush each tortilla with water. Cut each tortilla into eight wedges, and place on prepared pan. Bake 3 minutes, turn, and continue baking 3 minutes longer, or until crisp.

Crabmeat Dip

Sensational and simple describes my "signature entertaining recipe." It pays to live in Louisiana—there's no substitution for fresh lump crabmeat, pricey but definitely worth the cost. Recipe may be cut in half-but it seems I always have a large group at my house.

Makes 64 (2 tablespoon) servings

4 ounces reduced-fat cream cheese

1/4 cup light mayonnaise

1/4 cup nonfat plain yogurt or nonfat sour cream

1 bunch green onions, chopped

1 tablespoon Worcestershire sauce

Hearty dash hot pepper sauce

Salt and pepper to taste

2 pounds lump crabmeat, picked for shells

1. In bowl, combine cream cheese, mayonnaise, and yogurt with fork until mixed. Stir in green onion, Worcestershire sauce, hot sauce, salt and pepper.

2. Carefully fold in crabmeat. Refrigerate until serving.

Spicy Advice

Serve as a salad over mixed greens with sliced tomatoes and avocados

Crabmeat Dip

Mango Chutney Spread

**Nutritional information
per serving:**

Calories 71
Calories from fat 59%
Fat 5g
Saturated Fat 2g
Cholesterol 13mg
Sodium 105mg
Carbohydrate 6g
Dietary Fiber 0g
Sugars 5g
Protein 2g
Dietary Exchanges:
1/2 other carbohydrate, 1 fat

Surprisingly simple with six ingredients and you have this mild sweet, spicy, and salty spread, (opposite flavors attract) that tantalizes every taste bud in each bite. Serve with crackers.

Makes 16 (2 tablespoon) servings

1 (8-ounce) package reduced-fat
    cream cheese
1/2 teaspoon curry powder
2/3 cup mango chutney

1/4 cup chopped green onions
1/4 cup chopped pecans, toasted
4 slices cooked turkey bacon, crumbled

1. Mix together cream cheese and curry, spread on serving plate.
2. Carefully spread chutney over cream cheese layer.
3. Sprinkle with green onions, pecans and bacon. Cover, refrigerate until serving.

*Mango chutney is in the
grocery with jars of chutney
and sauces.*

Mango Chutney Spread

Feta Fruit Layered Loaf

Layers of tart cranberries, sweet apricots, feta, cream cheese, green onions and parsley create an eye-popping presentation, with a splendid blend of flavors.

Makes 15-20 servings

Nutritional information per serving:
Calories 87
Calories from fat 60%
Fat 6g
Saturated Fat 3g
Cholesterol 18mg
Sodium 127mg
Carbohydrate 6g
Dietary Fiber 1g
Sugars 5g
Protein 3g
Dietary Exchanges:
1/2 fruit, 1/2 very lean meat,
1 fat

2 (8-ounce) packages reduced-fat cream cheese

1/2 cup crumbled reduced-fat feta cheese

1/2 cup dried cranberries

2 tablespoons slivered almonds, toasted

1/2 cup chopped green onions

1/3 cup chopped parsley

1/2 cup dried chopped apricots

1. Line 8x4x2 loaf pan with plastic wrap, coat with nonstick cooking spray.

2. In mixing bowl, mix together cream cheese and feta, set aside.

3. In loaf pan begin layering with cranberries and almonds on bottom, one-third cream cheese mixture, green onions and parsley, one-third cream cheese mixture, apricots, one-third cream cheese mixture. Refrigerate until ready to serve.

4. To serve, turn pan upside down on serving plate and unmold, removing plastic wrap.

Spicy Advice

Serve with gingersnaps.

Spinach Feta Cheese Ball

A quick and easy make-ahead cheese ball with the perfect balance of Mediterranean flavors. Serve with crackers.

Makes 24 (2 tablespoon) servings

Nutritional information per serving:
Calories 41
Calories from fat 55%
Fat 3g
Saturated Fat 1g
Cholesterol 8mg
Sodium 111mg
Carbohydrate 2g
Dietary Fiber 1g
Sugars 1g
Protein 2g
Dietary Exchanges:
1/2 fat

1 (8-ounce) package reduced-fat cream cheese

1/2 cup crumbled reduced-fat feta cheese

1 (10-ounce) package frozen chopped spinach, thawed and squeezed dry

1 (14-ounce) can artichoke hearts, drained and chopped

1/2 cup sun-dried tomatoes, reconstituted in hot water

2 teaspoons minced garlic

Pepper to taste

1. In food processor or mixer, combine cream cheese and feta cheese. Add spinach, mix. Stir in artichokes, sun-dried tomatoes, garlic, and pepper until blended.

2. Form into a ball. Cover with plastic wrap, refrigerate until serving.

Remoulade Sauce

As quick as you turn on your food processor, this amazing New Orleans favorite Remoulade Sauce is made. Serve with shrimp, crabmeat or as a dressing over salad.

Makes 10 (2 tablespoon) servings

Nutritional information per serving:

Calories 43
Calories from fat 84%
Fat 4g
Saturated Fat 1g
Cholesterol 0mg
Sodium 153mg
Carbohydrate 2g
Dietary Fiber 1g
Sugars 1g
Protein 0g
Dietary Exchanges:
1 fat

1/3 cup Creole or grainy mustard

2 tablespoons prepared horseradish

1/4 cup chopped onions

1/4 cup chopped green onions

2 tablespoons chopped parsley

1 tablespoon paprika

1 teaspoon Worcestershire sauce

1 teaspoon minced garlic

3 tablespoons olive oil

3 tablespoons red wine vinegar

1. In food processor, combine mustard, horseradish, onion, green onions, parsley, paprika, Worcestshire sauce and garlic and pulse until blended.

2. With food processor on, pour olive oil in thin stream and continue to mix until thickened. Slowly add vinegar in thin stream and blend well.

Shrimp Remoulade

Watermelon Gazpacho

Nutritional information
per serving:
Calories 103
Calories from fat 36%
Fat 4g
Saturated Fat 1g
Cholesterol 0mg
Sodium 72mg
Carbohydrate 16g
Dietary Fiber 1g
Sugars 11g
Protein 1g
Dietary Exchanges:
1/2 fruit, 1 vegetable, 1 fat

An outstanding summer starter with surprise ingredients. One step to the most refreshing make-ahead soup. Refrigerate to let the flavors blend.

Makes 10 (1-cup) servings

8 cups seedless watermelon chunks

2 cucumbers, peeled, seeded and cut into chunks

1 small onion, chopped

1 (12-ounce) jar roasted red peppers, drained

1 cup chopped tomatoes

1/2 cup cranberry cocktail juice

3 tablespoons olive oil

1/4 cup raspberry vinegar

Salt to taste

Hearty dash hot sauce

1. Place all ingredients into food processor, pulse until almost pureed, depending on preference. Add more cranberry juice, if needed.

Watermelon and Tomato Salad

Nutritional information
per serving:
Calories 46
Calories from fat 29%
Fat 0g
Saturated Fat 0g
Cholesterol 0mg
Sodium 6mg
Carbohydrate 8g
Dietary Fiber 1g
Sugars 6g
Protein 1g
Dietary Exchanges:
1/2 fruit, 1/2 fat

Cool crisp watermelon, juicy tomatoes, and fresh basil with balsamic vinegar creates an extraordinary and invigorating light salad.

Makes 10 (1/2-cup) servings

4 cups scooped out watermelon balls or chunks

1/2 cup chopped red onion

1 pint cherry tomatoes, halved

2 tablespoons fresh chopped basil

1 tablespoon olive oil

2 tablespoons balsamic vinegar

Salt to taste

1. In bowl, combine watermelon, onion, tomatoes and basil. Whisk together oil and vinegar, toss with salad. Season to taste. Refrigerate until serving.

Spicy Advice

Toss in crumbled reduced-fat feta, if desired.

Strawberry and Kiwi Mixed Green Salad

Enliven a salad with strawberry and kiwi to add vivid colors and taste — toss with a light flavorful vinaigrette and your salad makes a statement!

Makes 6 - 8 servings

8 cups mixed greens (Bibb, red leaf, spinach)

1 1/2 cups sliced strawberries

2 kiwis, peeled and sliced

1 tablespoon sesame seeds

1 green onion, chopped

1/3 cup raspberry vinegar

2 teaspoons Dijon mustard

1/4 cup canola oil

Spiced walnuts, optional (page 122)

1. In large bowl, mix together greens, strawberries and kiwi.

2. In small bowl, whisk together sesame seeds, green onion, vinegar, Dijon mustard, and oil. Refrigerate vinaigrette until ready to use.

3. When ready to toss salad, add dressing gradually, serve immediately.

Spicy Advice

Top with Spicy Walnuts, page 122.

Strawberry and Kiwi Mixed Green Salad
with Spicy Walnuts

Mixed Greens with Apples and Cranberries with Cranberry Vinaigrette

Tart apples, sweet cranberries and toasted walnuts with a slightly sweet rich vinaigrette make this a quick toss together special salad.

Makes 6 servings

1 cup sliced tart apples

1/2 cup thinly sliced red onion

1/3 cup dried cranberries

1/3 cup chopped walnuts, toasted

6 cups mixed greens

1/4 cup crumbled reduced-fat feta cheese

Cranberry Vinaigrette, recipe follows

1. In bowl, combine apples, onion, cranberries, walnuts and mixed greens. Toss with feta and Cranberry Vinaigrette (see recipe). Serve.

Cranberry Vinaigrette

Use this fantastic vinaigrette on your favorite salad.

1 tablespoon honey

2 tablespoons cranberry cocktail juice

1/3 cup balsamic vinegar

1 teaspoon Dijon mustard

1 tablespoon olive oil

Salt and pepper to taste

2 tablespoons nonfat sour cream

In small bowl, whisk together honey, cranberry juice, vinegar, mustard, oil, and season to taste. Whisk in sour cream.

Bok Choy Salad

Introduce yourself to this versatile Chinese white cabbage, a leafy green vegetable, found in mainstream groceries for this innovative salad that everyone will surprisingly enjoy.

Makes 6 servings

2 bunches baby bok choy, cleaned and chopped or sliced (about 6 cups)

1 bunch green onions, chopped

1/4 cup sliced almonds, toasted

1 (8-ounce) can mandarin oranges, drained

2 tablespoons olive oil

3 tablespoons seasoned rice vinegar

1 tablespoon plus 1 teaspoon sugar

2 tablespoons low sodium soy sauce

1. In large bowl, combine bok choy, green onions, almonds and mandarin oranges.

2. In small bowl, whisk together olive oil, vinegar, sugar and soy sauce. Toss salad with dressing and serve.

Spicy Advice

A fall/winter member of the cabbage family, the flavor of Bok Choy is mild and slightly sweet with a gentle hint of cabbage. Only 30 calories a cup and good source of vitamins C and A and calcium.

Bok Choy Salad

Easy Edamame Salad

**Nutritional information
per serving:**

Calories 99
Calories from fat 46%
Fat 5g
Saturated Fat 1g
Cholesterol 4mg
Sodium 210mg
Carbohydrate 8g
Dietary Fiber 3g
Sugars 4g
Protein 6g
Dietary Exchanges:
1/2 starch, 1 lean meat,
1/2 fat

Refreshing mint, dill, tangy feta, and crunchy nutritious edamame create this simple super-star summer salad.

Makes 6 (1/2 cup) servings

1 1/2 cups shelled edamame

1 cup cherry tomatoes, halved

1/4 cup chopped green onions

2 tablespoons finely chopped
    fresh mint

1 teaspoon dried dill weed leaves

3 tablespoons seasoned rice vinegar

1 tablespoon olive oil

3 tablespoons crumbled reduced-fat
    feta cheese

Salt and pepper to taste

1. Cook edamame according to package directions. Drain, cool.

2. In bowl, add remaining ingredients to cooled edamame, toss together.

We've reached the age where
we just can't function without our
glasses...*especially if they're empty.*

Green Veggie Salad with Citrus Vinaigrette

Fresh veggies with sweet raisins, toasty pine nuts and bacon tossed with the mild citrus dressing create a super sassy salad for a salad combo or side.

Makes 11 (1 cup) servings

6 cups broccoli florets	1/4 cup golden raisins
1/2 pound fresh green beans, stemmed	1/4 cup pecans, toasted
1 (6-ounce) package baby spinach	4 strips center cut bacon, cooked crispy, crumbled
1 cup seedless green grapes	Citrus Vinaigrette (recipe follows)
1 bunch green onions, chopped	

1. In microwave-safe large bowl, combine broccoli and green beans with 1/4 cup water. Microwave 4 minutes, rinse with cold water, drain.

2. In large bowl, combine broccoli, green beans, spinach, grapes, and green onions. Before serving add raisins, pecans and bacon. Toss with Citrus Vinaigrette (see recipe). Serve.

Citrus Vinaigrette

Twist of orange and mustard give this vinaigrette punch.

1/3 cup orange juice	1 tablespoon olive oil
2 tablespoons lemon juice	1 teaspoon dry mustard
2 tablespoons balsamic vinegar	1 tablespoon honey

In small bowl, whisk together all ingredients.

Chicken Salad with Orange Dijon Vinaigrette

This quick toss-and-mix dazzling salad consists of rotessire or leftover chicken, crunchy pecans, Ramen noodles, and sweet grapes with an Orange Vinaigrette.

Makes 8 (1-cup) servings

1 (3-ounce) package chicken Ramen noodles

1/3 cup pecan halves

4 cups mixed greens

2 cups shredded Napa cabbage

3 cups cooked, diced skinless chicken breasts

1 cup red grapes, cut in half

1 bunch green onions, chopped

Orange Dijon Vinaigrette (recipe follows)

1. Break Ramen noodles into small pieces and discard seasoning mix. In nonstick skillet coated with nonstick cooking spray, cook Ramen noodle pieces and pecans over medium heat, stirring until light brown, 3-4 minutes. Set aside.

2. In large bowl, combine mixed greens, Napa cabbage, chicken breast, grapes and green onions. When ready to serve, toss with Orange Dijon Vinaigrette (see recipe) and Ramen pecan mixture.

Orange Dijon Vinaigrette

Orange infused vinaigrette adds a touch of natural sweetness.

1/4 cup seasoned rice vinegar

2 tablespoons olive oil

1/4 cup orange juice

1 tablespoon honey

1 tablespoon Dijon mustard

Salt and pepper to taste

In small bowl, whisk together all ingredients.

Mediterranean Chicken Spinach Salad

Nutritional information per serving:

Calories 204
Calories from fat 37%
Fat 8g
Saturated Fat 2g
Cholesterol 45mg
Sodium 452mg
Carbohydrate 12g
Dietary Fiber 4g
Sugars 5g
Protein 20g
Dietary Exchanges:
2 vegetable, 2 1/2 lean meat

With the magic of Rotessire chicken and chic ingredients, edamame, sun-dried tomatoes, mint, and feta, you have a satisfying, stylish light entrée salad. Fresh mint makes a difference – if you don't have it growing rampant, check any grocery.

Makes 6 servings (3/4-1 cup chicken, 1/2 cup spinach)

2 cups diced, rotessire skinless chicken breast

1 cup edamame, cooked according to package directions

1/2 cup chopped sun-dried tomatoes, reconstituted

1 bunch green onions, chopped

1 cucumber, peeled and chopped

1/4 cup chopped fresh mint leaves or 1 tablespoon dried mint

2 teaspoons dried dill weed leaves

3 tablespoons roasted garlic seasoned rice vinegar or any vinegar

1 tablespoon lemon juice

2 tablespoons olive oil

3 cups packed baby spinach leaves

1/3 cup crumbled reduced-fat feta cheese

Instead of spinach, you can toss chicken mixture with quick cooking couscous for another great option.

1. In large bowl, combine chicken, edamame, sun-dried tomatoes, green onions, cucumber, mint, and dill, mixing well.

2. In small bowl, whisk together vinegar, lemon juice, and olive oil. Toss with spinach and feta and divide mixture evenly among individual plates. Top with chicken mixture. Serve.

Mediterranean Chicken Spinach Salad

Festive Pasta Salad

A unique combination of taste, texture and vibrancy with a blast of flavor and eye-catching colors. A group gathering salad that makes a lot, and I was flooded with compliments and recipe requests.

Makes 28 (1/2 cup servings)

1 (16-ounce) package tri-colored bow tie pasta

3 cups broccoli florets

1 cup shredded or finely chopped carrots

1 bunch green onions, chopped

1/2 cup shelled edamame, cooked according to package directions

1/3 cup sliced Kalamata olives

1/2 cup sesame seeds, toasted

1/2 cup chopped walnuts

1/2 cup dried cranberries

1/3-1/2 cup Light Raspberry and Walnut Dressing or light dressing of choice

1. Cook pasta according to package directions, drain.

2. In large bowl, combine all ingredients except dressing. Toss with dressing.

Nutritional information per serving:

Calories 117
Calories from fat 29%
Fat 4g
Saturated Fat 0g
Cholesterol 0mg
Sodium 38mg
Carbohydrate 17g
Dietary Fiber 2g
Sugars 4g
Protein 4g
Dietary Exchanges:
1 starch, 1/2 fat

Spicy Advice

One pound of pasta (uncooked) will yield 4 cups cooked pasta. Add cooked chicken or shrimp for a heartier version.

Crab Mango Salad

Sweet mango, red peppers, green onions and crabmeat with crunchy cashews create an exciting combination. May serve with crackers as a dip. Shrimp may be substituted for the crabmeat.

Makes 7 (1/2-cup) servings

1 teaspoon canola oil

1/2 cup finely chopped red bell pepper

2 cups finely chopped mangoes

1/3 cup chopped green onions

1/4 cup part-skim ricotta cheese

1 tablespoon lemon juice

Pinch cayenne

Salt and pepper to taste

1 pound lump crabmeat, picked for shells

1/3 cup chopped cashews

1. In small nonstick skillet, heat oil and sauté red pepper until tender

2. In large bowl, combine red pepper, mangoes, green onions, ricotta, lemon juice, cayenne and season to taste. Fold in crabmeat and cashews.

Nutritional information per serving:

Calories 161
Calories from fat 29%
Fat 5g
Saturated Fat 1g
Cholesterol 53mg
Sodium 261mg
Carbohydrate 12g
Dietary Fiber 1g
Sugars 8g
Protein 17g
Dietary Exchanges:
1 fruit, 2 1/2 lean meat

Cranberry Crush

Nutritional information per serving:

Calories 66
Calories from fat 0%
Fat 0g
Saturated Fat 0g
Cholesterol 3mg
Sodium 21mg
Carbohydrate 16g
Dietary Fiber 2g
Sugars 11g
Protein 1g
Dietary Exchanges:
1 other carbohydrate

The ultimate make-ahead holiday cranberry sauce with a little kick, from my friend Jane-one taste is all it takes. Also, great served with meat.

Makes 12 (1/4-cup) servings

1 small onion, cut in chunks
1 (12-ounce) package fresh cranberries
1/2 cup sugar

3/4 cup nonfat sour cream
2 tablespoons prepared horseradish

1. In food processor, process onion until chopped. Add cranberries, sugar, sour cream and horseradish and process until almost pureed.

2. Place in freezable container and freeze overnight. Remove from freezer 3 hours to soften. Serve and refrigerate leftovers.

Cranberries freeze up to one year.

Cranberry Crush

Lemon Pie

Medium-Dark Roast

So simple, yet divine, a cross between a cheesecake and pie. Serve with fresh berries.

Makes 8-10 servings

1 (8-ounce) package reduced-fat cream cheese

1 (14-ounce) can fat-free sweetened condensed milk

1/2 cup lemon juice

1 tablespoon grated lemon rind

1 (9-inch) prepared graham cracker crust

1. In mixing bowl, mix together cream cheese, sweetened condensed milk, and lemon juice until smooth and creamy. Stir in lemon rind.

2. Transfer to graham cracker crust. Refrigerate until firm, 4 hours.

Nutritional information per serving:

Calories 261
Calories from fat 34%
Fat 10g
Saturated Fat 4g
Cholesterol 19mg
Sodium 213mg
Carbohydrate 37g
Dietary Fiber 0g
Sugars 29g
Protein 6g
Dietary Exchanges:
2 1/2 other carbohydrate,
1 very lean meat, 1 1/2 fat

Spicy Advice

Try using a gingersnap crust (I love ginger snaps) which complements the luscious lemon flavor.

Lemon Pie

Quickies

A woman is like a tea bag:
**you cannot tell how strong she is
until you put her in hot water.**

-Nancy Reagan

Feta Crumble Dip

These few ingredients in this simple "knock-out" dip create an explosion of fresh flavors for a captivating combination. Serve with crackers. Leftovers can be used as a condiment on sandwiches or with chicken or fish.

Makes 8 (1/4 cup) servings

3 tablespoons olive oil

2 tablespoons balsamic vinegar

1 tablespoon lemon juice

1/2 cup chopped green onions

1/2 cup finely chopped fresh parsley

2 tablespoons chopped sun-dried tomatoes (reconstituted)

Salt and pepper to taste

1 (4-ounce) package reduced-fat feta cheese, crumbled

1. In bowl, combine all ingredients, except feta mixing well. Toss with feta, refrigerate up to one hour, serve.

Nutritional information per serving:

Calories 80
Calories from fat 73%
Fat 7g
Saturated Fat 2g
Cholesterol 5mg
Sodium 193mg
Carbohydrate 3g
Dietary Fiber 0g
Sugars 1g
Protein 3g
Dietary Exchanges:
1/2 lean meat, 1 fat

Spicy Advice

To reconstitute sun-dried tomatoes, pour hot water over and let sit for 10 minutes. Drain.

Feta Crumble Dip

Watermelon and Feta Salsa

Nutritional information per serving:

Calories 29
Calories from fat 36%
Fat 1g
Saturated Fat 0g
Cholesterol 1mg
Sodium 98mg
Carbohydrate 4g
Dietary Fiber 0g
Sugars 3g
Protein 1g
Dietary Exchanges:
1/2 fruit

An unusual combination, yet, one of my summer favorites with sweet watermelon, fresh mint, salty olives, and feta bursting with sweet and salty in each mouthful.

Makes 16 (1/4) cup servings

4 cups chopped watermelon

1/2 cup chopped red onion

1/3 cup crumbled reduced-fat feta cheese

1/4 cup chopped fresh mint

2 tablespoons chopped Kalamata olives

2 tablespoons seasoned rice vinegar

2 teaspoons olive oil

1 In small bowl mix together all ingredients. Serve.

Spicy Advice

Try the red pepper seasoned rice vinegar for a little extra zing. Raid a salad bar for fresh Kalamata olives-it makes a difference.

Watermelon and Feta Salad

Edamame Dip

You'll keep people guessing with this explosively flavored fantastic dip. Serve with pita chips or try using green, red and yellow pepper squares as chips.

8 (1/4-cup) servings

2 cups frozen shelled edamame

2 garlic cloves

Salt

1/2 teaspoon ground cumin

1/2 cup chopped fresh parsley

1/3 cup lemon juice

1/3 cup water

1 tablespoon sesame oil

1. Prepare edamame according to package directions.

2. In food processor, pulse edamame and garlic until coarsely chopped. Add remaining ingredients and process until smooth. If needed, add more water for a creamier consistency.

Spicy Advice

If recipe calls for a larger amount of parsley, fresh is best!

Special Caesar Salad

Make the dressing, toast the sesame seeds and toss together when ready to serve. You'll love the flair of sesame seeds and a creamy healthier Caesar dressing.

Makes 6 servings

1/3 cup nonfat plain yogurt

2 tablespoons lemon juice

1 teaspoon olive oil

1 teaspoon vinegar

1 teaspoon Dijon mustard

1 teaspoon Worcestershire sauce

1/2 teaspoon minced garlic

1 large head romaine lettuce, torn into pieces

1/4 cup grated Parmesan cheese

2 tablespoons sesame seeds, toasted

1. In small bowl, whisk together yogurt, lemon juice, olive oil, vinegar, mustard, Worcestershire sauce, and garlic; set aside.

2. In bowl, combine lettuce, Parmesan cheese and sesame seeds. Toss with dressing.

Chicken/Turkey Apricot Rice Salad

Nutritional information per serving:

Calories 277
Calories from fat 23%
Fat 7g
Saturated Fat 1g
Cholesterol 30mg
Sodium 111mg
Carbohydrate 39g
Dietary Fiber 4g
Sugars 19g
Protein 16g
Dietary Exchanges:
1 1/2 starch, 1 fruit,
2 lean meat

Holiday time and extra wild rice and turkey? Turn leftovers into another meal by spiking the rice with vivid colors, flavors and crunchy almonds for an undemanding and unforgettable salad. Rotisserie or pre-cooked, grilled chicken fillets are great short cuts to enjoy year round.

Makes 8 (1 cup) servings

2 tablespoons lime juice

2 tablespoons roasted garlic seasoned rice vinegar

2 tablespoons olive oil

1 tablespoon honey

1/2 teaspoon ground ginger

4 cups cooked wild or brown rice

2 cups chopped boneless skinless cooked chicken breasts or turkey

1 cup dried apricots strips (about 6 ounce package)

1/2 cup dried cranberries

1 cup chopped green onions

1/3 cup sliced almonds, toasted

1. In small bowl, whisk together lime juice, vinegar, oil, honey and ginger; set aside.

2. In large bowl, combine remaining ingredients except almonds. Combine with dressing and toss with almonds. Serve.

Use kitchen scissors to cut dried fruit into strips or even cut your meat or chicken.

Chicken/Turkey Apricot Rice Salad

Pull Apart Bread

This amazing buttery tasting bread will quickly become the talk of the meal. It takes minutes to make and every time I serve this bread, people go crazy about my homemade pull apart bread---shhhh!

Makes 12-16 servings

3 tablespoons butter, melted

3 (8-ounce) cans reduced-fat
    crescent rolls

1. Preheat oven 375°F.

2. Pour butter into bottom of nonstick Bundt pan. Unroll crescent rolls into four rectangles (two triangular shapes) and roll up (like cigar). Layer on top the butter overlapping the rolls.

3. Bake 19-23 minutes or until top is golden brown. Immediately invert onto serving plate.

Pull Apart Bread

Crunchy Fish with Lemon Sauce

Nutritional information per serving:

Calories 283
Calories from fat 38%
Fat 12g
Saturated Fat 3g
Cholesterol 94mg
Sodium 98mg
Carbohydrate 10g
Dietary Fiber 0g
Sugars 0g
Protein 32g
Dietary Exchanges:
1/2 starch, 4 lean meat

Panko bread crumbs, a coarser crumb, gives this fish a wonderful crunchy crust-great new choice of coating. Serve with or without Lemon Sauce.

Makes 6 servings

2 pounds trout or catfish fillets (mild fish)
Salt and pepper to taste
4 tablespoons lemon juice, divided
1 cup panko bread crumbs
2 tablespoons cornstarch

2 tablespoons olive oil
1 tablespoon butter
1/3 cup fat-free chicken broth
1 tablespoon chopped parsley

1. In bowl, season fish with salt and pepper and 2 tablespoons lemon juice. In plastic bag, combine bread crumbs and cornstarch. Add fish; shake to coat fish with mixture, pressing mixture onto fish.

2. In large nonstick skillet, heat oil over medium high heat, add fish cooking 4 - 5 minutes on each side or until fish is flaky.

3. Remove fish to serving plate, add butter to pan. After butter is melted, add chicken broth and remaining 2 tablespoons lemon juice, scraping pan of any bits to add flavor. Add parsley. Heat 2 minutes, serve with fish.

Panko bread crumbs are found with regular bread crumbs at grocery.

Crunchy Fish with Lemon Sauce

Terrific Tilapia

Medium-Dark Roast

Restaurant quality in presentation and preparation in the comfort of your own home. I literally threw this together in minutes while sipping on a glass of wine! An ideal spring dish but you can substitute any seasonal vegetable for the asparagus.

Makes 4 servings

2 tablespoons all-purpose flour

1 teaspoon dried oregano leaves

2 tablespoons chopped parsley

4 (6-ounce) tilapia fillets

Salt and pepper to taste

2 tablespoons olive oil

1/2 teaspoon minced garlic

1 cup sliced mushrooms

1 cup cherry tomatoes, halved

1 cup fresh asparagus tips

1/4 cup lemon juice

1/3 cup fat-free chicken broth

1. In shallow dish, combine flour, oregano and parsley. Season fish to taste.

2. In large nonstick skillet over medium-high heat, heat olive oil. Dredge fish in flour mixture, shaking off the excess and cook in skillet until golden brown, about 4 minutes. Turn over and cook several more minutes, or until fish is flaky. Transfer to a plate and keep warm.

3. In same skillet, add garlic, mushrooms, tomatoes, and asparagus, stirring, about 1 minute. Stir in lemon juice and broth, and continue cooking until asparagus are crisp tender. Serve fish with sauce and vegetables on top.

Nutritional information per serving:

Calories 267
Calories from fat 33%
Fat 10g
Saturated Fat 2g
Cholesterol 85mg
Sodium 130mg
Carbohydrate 9g
Dietary Fiber 2g
Sugars 3g
Protein 37g
Dietary Exchanges:
1 vegetable, 5 lean meat

Spicy Advice

Keep it convenient! Always have a jar of minced garlic and bottle of lemon juice in the refrigerator.

Make thyme to live, laugh and...love.

Salmon Marsala

Nutritional information per serving:

Calories 241
Calories from fat 30%
Fat 8g
Saturated Fat 1g
Cholesterol 65mg
Sodium 162mg
Carbohydrate 10g
Dietary Fiber 2g
Sugars 5g
Protein 27g
Dietary Exchanges:
1/2 other carbohydrate,
3 lean meat

Looking to impress, but no time to cook? Salmon with Marsala wine and mushrooms have a sophisticated earthly flavor in this easy recipe.

Makes 4 servings

1 tablespoons olive oil

1 onion, thinly sliced

1 teaspoon minced garlic

1/2 pound sliced mushrooms

4 (4-ounce) skinless salmon fillets

1/3 cup Marsala wine or cooking wine

3/4 cup fat-free chicken broth

3 teaspoons cornstarch

1. In large nonstick skillet, heat oil and sauté onion, garlic, and mushrooms until tender.

2. Add salmon to skillet, cooking 4 minutes, turn onto other side. Meanwhile, in small bowl, mix together wine, broth and cornstarch.

3. When salmon is almost done, add wine mixture to the salmon. Stir gently, as mixture thickens quickly.

Salmon Marsala

Barbecue Shrimp

Nutritional information per serving:

Calories 179
Calories from fat 40%
Fat 8g
Saturated Fat 1g
Cholesterol 168mg
Sodium 398mg
Carbohydrate 4g
Dietary Fiber 1g
Sugars 2g
Protein 19g
Dietary Exchanges:
3 lean meat

Words can't describe this Louisiana favorite with its superb sauce! Here's my lazy version using peeled shrimp but equally as good. Serve with French bread and angel hair pasta to not miss one drop of sauce.

Makes 2-4 servings

2 tablespoons olive oil

2 tablespoons fat-free Caesar or creamy Italian dressing

1 tablespoon minced garlic

1/4 teaspoon cayenne

2 tablespoons Worcestershire sauce

1 teaspoon paprika

1 teaspoon dried oregano leaves

1 teaspoon dried thyme leaves

Salt and pepper to taste

1 pound medium-large peeled shrimp

1/3 cup white wine or cooking wine

1. In large nonstick skillet, combine oil, dressing, garlic, cayenne, Worcestershire sauce, paprika, oregano, thyme, and season to taste, cooking over medium heat until sauce begins to boil.

2. Add shrimp, cook several minutes, stirring. Add wine, cook another 5 minutes or until shrimp are done.

Barbecue Shrimp

Mediterranean Shrimp

Serve this versatile recipe with toasted sliced French bread as an appetizer or combine with pasta for an entree, either way; you'll enjoy this amazing recipe.

Makes 4 (3/4-cup) servings

Nutritional information per serving:

Calories 219
Calories from fat 43%
Fat 10g
Saturated Fat 2g
Cholesterol 171mg
Sodium 758mg
Carbohydrate 10g
Dietary Fiber 3g
Sugars 3g
Protein 21g
Dietary Exchanges:
2 vegetable, 3 lean meat

1 tablespoon olive oil

1 tablespoon minced garlic

1 bunch green onions, chopped

1 pound small peeled shrimp

1/2 cup halved Kalamata olives

1/2 cup coarsely chopped sun-dried tomatoes (reconstituted)

2 tablespoons lemon juice

1/2 cup clam juice or fat-free chicken broth

1 teaspoon dried basil or 1 tablespoon freshly chopped basil

Salt and pepper

1/4 cup crumbled reduced-fat feta cheese

2 tablespoons chopped parsley

1. In large nonstick skillet, heat olive oil, and sauté garlic and green onions, one minute. Add shrimp, cooking until shrimp are almost done.

2. Add olives and sun-dried tomatoes, cook one minute.

3. Add lemon juice, clam juice, and basil, bring to a boil, reduce heat, and simmer few minutes. Season to taste, add feta and chopped parsley.

When olives are a key ingredient, raid a salad or olive bar for high quality olives.

Crab Tacos

Tacos stuffed with a mild creamy crab mixture, fresh tomatoes and cucumbers make a speedy, spectacular light meal, especially enjoyable on hot days.

Makes 8 tacos (about 1/3 cup filling and 3 tablespoons tomato mixture)

3 tablespoons light mayonnaise

2 tablespoons nonfat sour cream

1/4 cup chopped red onion

1 tablespoon chopped jarred jalapenos

2 tablespoons lime juice, divided

1/2 teaspoon minced garlic

1/4 teaspoon ground cumin

Salt and pepper to taste

1 pound lump crabmeat, picked for shells

1 1/2 cups chopped tomatoes

1/2 cup chopped peeled cucumbers

1 teaspoon olive oil

8 corn taco shells, heated according to directions

Chopped avocados, optional

1. In bowl, mix together mayonnaise, sour cream, onion, jalapeno, 1 tablespoon lime juice, garlic and cumin. Season to taste. Carefully fold in crabmeat. Refrigerate until ready to assemble.

2. In bowl, combine tomatoes, cucumbers, remaining 1 tablespoon lime juice and olive oil. Season to taste. Refrigerate.

3. Fill heated taco shells with crabmeat, tomato mixture, and avocados, if desired.

Crab Tacos

Chicken with Olives, Tomato and Basil

Nutritional information per serving:

Calories 237
Calories from fat 15%
Fat 4g
Saturated Fat 1g
Cholesterol 99mg
Sodium 224mg
Carbohydrate 9g
Dietary Fiber 2g
Sugars 4g
Protein 41g
Dietary Exchanges:
2 vegetable,
5 very lean meat

Here's a one skillet quick chicken recipe with fresh ingredients that infuse the chicken with incredible flavor. Best if use Kalamata olives and fresh basil.

Makes 4 servings

1 1/2 pounds boneless, skinless chicken breasts (pounded thin if desired)

1 teaspoon paprika

Salt and pepper to taste

1/4 cup lemon juice

1/4 cup chopped onion

1 teaspoon minced garlic

1 pint grape tomatoes, halved

1/3 cup sliced Kalamata olives

1/4 cup chopped fresh basil or 1 tablespoon dried basil leaves

1/3 cup chopped Italian parsley

1. Sprinkle chicken with paprika, salt and pepper; drizzle with lemon juice.

2. In large nonstick skillet over medium heat, coated with nonstick cooking spray, cook chicken on each side until chicken is golden, about 3-5 minutes each side.

3. Add onion, garlic, tomatoes and olives, cooking for several minutes or until tomatoes begin to soften. Sprinkle with basil and parsley before serving.

Spicy Advice

Italian (flat leaf) parsley has more flavor than curly parsley and is better for cooking. You can freeze parsley!

Chicken with Olives, Tomato and Basil

Home-Style Chicken

Nutritional information per serving:

Calories 272
Calories from fat 10%
Fat 3g
Saturated Fat 1g
Cholesterol 99mg
Sodium 654mg
Carbohydrate 15g
Dietary Fiber 1g
Sugars 2g
Protein 41g
Dietary Exchanges:
1 starch, 5 very lean meat

Nothing beats tradition! Smothered chicken in a tasty gravy goes great with rice or potatoes.

Makes 4 servings

1 1/2 pounds boneless, skinless chicken breasts

Salt and pepper to taste

1/4 cup all-purpose flour

1/2 cup chopped onion

1/2 cup chopped green bell pepper

1 (1.25-ounce) package Onion Soup mix (one envelope)

1 1/4 cups water plus 2 tablespoons water, divided

1/3 cup white wine or chicken broth

1 tablespoon cornstarch

1. Season chicken and coat lightly with flour.

2. In large nonstick skillet coated with nonstick cooking spray, brown chicken on both sides, remove from skillet. Add onion and green pepper, scraping sides and sautéing until tender.

3. Return chicken to skillet. In small bowl, combine soup mix, 1 1/4 cups water, and wine. Pour over chicken. Bring to boil, reduce heat, and cook, covered, until chicken is tender, 20-25 minutes.

4. In small bowl, mix cornstarch and remaining 2 tablespoons water, add to sauce in pan. Bring to boil and boil one minute, stirring until thickened. Serve chicken and sauce.

Spicy Advice

Always remember to dissolve cornstarch in cold liquid before adding to your recipe-cornstarch is a quick thickening agent.

Quick Chicken and Artichokes ❄

Nutritional information per serving:

Calories 301
Calories from fat 28%
Fat 9g
Saturated Fat 2g
Cholesterol 99mg
Sodium 336mg
Carbohydrate 11g
Dietary Fiber 1g
Sugars 1g
Protein 42g
Dietary Exchanges:
1/2 starch, 1 vegetable,
5 lean meat

Chicken, dill and artichokes create a quick, toss together pizzaz pleasing dish.

Makes 4 servings

1/4 cup all-purpose flour

Salt and pepper to taste

1 1/2 pounds boneless, skinless chicken breasts, cut into strips

2 tablespoons olive oil

1/2 cup fat-free chicken broth

1 tablespoon lemon juice

1 teaspoon dried dill weed leaves

1 (14.5-ounce) can artichoke heart quarters, drained

1. In small plate, combine flour with salt and pepper; coat chicken strips.

2. In large nonstick skillet, heat olive oil and cook chicken over medium high heat, until lightly browned on each side, stirring, 5-7 minutes.

3. Add broth, scraping sides of pan, reduce heat, and add lemon juice and dill. Add artichokes; continue cooking 5 minutes longer or until chicken is tender.

Open Face Pulled Chicken Sandwiches ❄

Nutritional information per serving:

Calories 220
Calories from fat 12%
Fat 3g
Saturated Fat 1g
Cholesterol 66mg
Sodium 429mg
Carbohydrate 20g
Dietary Fiber 2g
Sugars 8g
Protein 29g
Dietary Exchanges:
1 starch, 1/2 other carbohydrate,
3 very lean meat

Move over pulled pork, this chicken has a perfectly balanced tangy and sweet savory barbecue sauce. Serve with your favorite barbecue condiments—I like red onions and pickles. Try with Brie, for a fantastic addition.

Makes 4 servings with 1/2 cup pulled chicken

1/4 cup ketchup

1 tablespoon cider vinegar

1 tablespoon Dijon mustard

1 tablespoon molasses

1 teaspoon chili powder

1/2 teaspoon ground cumin

1/8 teaspoon ground ginger

1 pound chicken breast tenders, cut into chunks

2 whole wheat buns, split and toasted

1. In medium pot, combine all ingredients except chicken. Bring to boil, add chicken. Reduce heat, cover, and cook, stirring occasionally until chicken is tender, 20-25 minutes.

2. When chicken is fall-apart tender, shred chicken using two forks. Pile on toasted buns.

Spicy Advice

Try serving over Sweet Potato Cornmeal Biscuits (see recipe page 154)

Speedy Chicken Chili

I had salsa, kidney and navy beans, and chicken so what could be better than a chicken chili? Serve with reduced-fat cheese, avocado, and onions.

Makes 10 (1-cup) servings

Nutritional information per serving:

Calories 257
Calories from fat 7%
Fat 2g
Saturated Fat 0g
Cholesterol 53mg
Sodium 740mg
Carbohydrate 29g
Dietary Fiber 7g
Sugars 6g
Protein 29g
Dietary Exchanges:
2 starch, 4 very lean meat

2 pounds boneless, skinless chicken breasts, cubed

Salt and pepper to taste

2 cups salsa

1 (14 1/2-ounce) can chopped tomatoes, with juice

4 cups fat-free chicken broth

1 (4-ounce) can chopped green chilies

2 teaspoon dried oregano leaves

1 teaspoon ground cumin

2 cups frozen corn, thawed

1 (15-ounce) can red kidney beans, rinsed and drained

1 (15-ounce) can navy beans, rinsed and drained

Shredded reduced-fat cheese, avocado, and red onions, optional

1. In large pot coated with nonstick cooking spray, season chicken and cook until lightly browned, 5 minutes.

2. Add salsa, tomatoes, broth, green chilies, oregano, and cumin. Bring to boil, reduce heat, and cook 15 minutes. Add corn and beans, cooking another 5-10 minutes until well heated and bubbly. Serve with condiments.

Spicy Advice

Look for fresh salsa or your favorite flavored salsa to pump up flavor. For a short-cut, use pre-cooked, grilled whole chicken breast fillets (great grilled flavor) or rotisserie chicken.

Speedy Chicken Chili

Marinated Flank Steak

Dark Roast

Nutritional information per serving:

Calories 227
Calories from fat 36%
Fat 9g
Saturated Fat 4g
Cholesterol 64mg
Sodium 575mg
Carbohydrate 1g
Dietary Fiber 0g
Sugars 0g
Protein 33g
Dietary Exchanges:
4 1/2 lean meat

Nothing is simpler and better tasting than flank steak. Marinate in the morning and toss on the grill in the evening for a great entrée. Also, great meat for fajitas.

Makes 6 servings

2 pounds flank steak, trimmed of excess fat

Pepper to taste

2/3 cup low sodium soy sauce

1 tablespoon finely chopped fresh ginger

1 tablespoon honey

1 bunch green onions, chopped

1 teaspoon dried red pepper flakes

1 tablespoon minced garlic

1 tablespoon sesame oil

1. Season meat with pepper. In resealable plastic bag or glass oblong dish, mix together soy sauce, ginger, honey, green onions, red pepper flakes, garlic and oil. Add meat.

2. Cover, marinate in refrigerator 2 hours or overnight, turning occasionally. Discard marinade. Grill, covered, over hot fire 5 - 7 minutes on each side. Serve rare, cut diagonally across grain into thin slices. May be cooked in oven.

Perfect Pork Tenderloin

Nutritional information per serving:

Calories 129
Calories from fat 18%
Fat 2g
Saturated Fat 1g
Cholesterol 74mg
Sodium 255mg
Carbohydrate 0g
Dietary Fiber 0g
Sugars 0g
Protein 24g
Dietary Exchanges:
3 very lean meat

Here's my perfect 3 ingredient marinade for that last minute meal. You can freeze pork tenderloins in marinade to pull out when needed.

Makes 6-8 servings

1/4 cup low sodium soy sauce

1/4 cup roasted garlic seasoned rice vinegar

2 tablespoons honey

2 (1-pound) pork tenderloins, trimmed of excess fat

1. Combine all ingredients except tenderloins in resealable plastic bag. Add tenderloins and refrigerate overnight, if time permits.

2. Preheat oven 350°F. Bake 40-45 minutes or until meat thermometer inserted into thickest portion of tenderloin registers 160°F or can grill.

Sausage and Roasted Red Pepper Pizza ❄

Nutritional information per serving:

Calories 196
Calories from fat 37%
Fat 8g
Saturated Fat 3g
Cholesterol 19mg
Sodium 412mg
Carbohydrate 21g
Dietary Fiber 1g
Sugars 1g
Protein 11g
Dietary Exchanges:
1 1/2 starch, 1 lean meat, 1 fat

Sausage, roasted red peppers, spinach and mozzarella make this a simple upscale pizza.

Makes 8 slices

1 (12-inch) thin pizza crust

1 tablespoon olive oil

1 tablespoon minced garlic

4 ounces chicken sausage or gourmet sausage of choice, cut in thin slices

2 cups fresh baby spinach

1/2 cup roasted red pepper slices, drained (found in jar)

1/2 cup red onion thin slices, cut in half

1 cup shredded part-skim mozzarella cheese

1. Preheat oven 425°F. Coat crust with oil and garlic.

2. In a small nonstick skillet coated with nonstick cooking spray, cook sausage until lightly browned and done. Add spinach, stirring only until wilted.

3. Evenly spoon spinach mixture over crust and top with remaining ingredients. Bake 8–10 minutes, or until cheese is melted and crust is done.

Splurge with fresh mozzarella cheese for an added flavor value. Look for different varieties of sausauge from chicken to vegetarian.

Sausage and Roasted Red Pepper Pizza

Chicken Scampi Penne

An easy throw-together one-meal dish with a few surprise ingredients to jazz it up.

Makes 4 servings

1 1/2 pounds chicken breast tenders
Salt and pepper
2 tablespoons olive oil
1/2 cup chopped red onion
1 teaspoon minced garlic
2 tablespoons all-purpose flour
1 cup fat-free chicken broth

2 tablespoons lemon juice
1/3 cup white wine or cooking wine
3 tablespoons capers, drained
1/3 cup chopped parsley
8 ounces penne pasta
1/3 cup coarsely chopped avocado
1/4 cup grated Parmesan cheese

1. Season chicken to taste. In large nonstick skillet, heat oil and cook chicken until golden brown, about 5-6 minutes. Remove chicken from pan; set aside.

2. Add onion and garlic, stir 1 minute. Add flour, stirring 1 minute. Gradually add broth, lemon juice and wine, stirring. Bring to boil, reduce heat, cooking until slightly thickened. Return chicken to pan and add capers and parsley.

3. Meanwhile, cook pasta according to package instructions. Drain and toss with chicken mixture. Sprinkle with avocado and Parmesan cheese, and serve.

Spicy Advice

*Try using whole wheat
or multi-grain blend pastas
to boost fiber.*

Of course I don't look busy...
I did it right the first time!

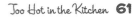

Sweet Potato Fantastic Fries

Just when I thought I couldn't create a better Sweet Potato Fry recipe!

Makes 4 servings

2 pounds Louisiana yams (sweet potatoes), about 2-3, peeled and cut into 4-inch long and 1/4-1/2-inch thick fries

2 tablespoons olive oil

2 teaspoons paprika

1 teaspoon chili powder

Salt and pepper to taste

1. Preheat oven 450°F. Line baking sheet with foil; coat with nonstick cooking spray.

2. Toss sweet potato fries with olive oil. In small bowl, mix together paprika, chili powder, and season to taste. Toss with fries.

3. Arrange in single layer on prepared pan. Bake 20 minutes on middle rack until potatoes begin to soften. Move pan to upper rack of oven; continue baking 10-15 minutes longer, until fries begin to crisp.

Nutritional information per serving:

Calories 248
Calories from fat 25%
Fat 7g
Saturated Fat 1g
Cholesterol 0mg
Sodium 124mg
Carbohydrate 44g
Dietary Fiber 7g
Sugars 9g
Protein 4g
Dietary Exchanges:
3 starch

Spicy Advice

For southwestern spicy sweet fry: 1 tablespoon sugar, 1 teaspoon ground cumin, and 1 teaspoon chili powder.

Great Fresh Green Beans

No intimidation with fresh green beans as this trouble-free recipe takes green beans from traditional to trendy in a flash with toasty pecans and light lemon essence.

Makes 4 servings

1 pound fresh green beans

1 tablespoon olive oil

1/4 cup chopped pecans

1 tablespoon lemon juice

Salt and pepper to taste

1. Place green beans in microwave-safe dish with little water, cover and microwave 4-5 minutes or until crisp tender. Drain and transfer to serving dish.

2. Meanwhile, in nonstick skillet, heat olive oil and cook pecans, over medium heat, stirring until golden brown. Add pecans and lemon juice to green beans. Season to taste.

Nutritional information per serving:

Calories 113
Calories from fat 61%
Fat 8g
Saturated Fat 1g
Cholesterol 0mg
Sodium 7mg
Carbohydrate 9g
Dietary Fiber 5g
Sugars 2g
Protein 3g
Dietary Exchanges:
2 vegetable, 1 1/2 fat

Brussels Sprouts Stir

Don't pass up this understated and underrated vegetable; if you have never had fresh Brussels sprouts you are in for a taste sensation with this simple recipe.

Makes 4 servings

1 pound Brussels sprouts

3 tablespoons olive oil, divided

1/2 cup chopped onion

Salt and pepper to taste

Crushed red pepper flakes

Nutritional information per serving:

Calories 146
Calories from fat 60%
Fat 10g
Saturated Fat 1g
Cholesterol 0mg
Sodium 29mg
Carbohydrate 12g
Dietary Fiber 5g
Sugars 3g
Protein 4g
Dietary Exchanges:
2 vegetable, 2 fat

1. Cut ends off Brussels sprouts and slice in half.

2. In medium nonstick skillet coated with nonstick cooking spray, heat 1 tablespoon olive oil, and sauté onion about 5 minutes or until tender. Remove from pan.

3. In same pan coated with nonstick cooking spray, heat remaining 2 tablespoons olive oil, and place Brussels sprout halves face down in skillet until golden brown, around 5 minutes. Return onions to skillet, and cook about 10 minutes, stirring occasionally, until tender. Season to taste.

Brussels Sprouts Stir

Fudgy Brownie Pie

Dark Roast

This fudgy rich brownie dessert looks like it came from the bakery, but is so simply made with brownie mix, instant pudding and whipped topping with coffee enhancing the chocolate flavor-the perfect chocoholic finish to any meal.

Makes 10 servings

1/3 cup warm water

1 1/2 teaspoons instant dark roast or espresso coffee, divided

1 (19.85-ounce) box fudge brownie mix

1 egg

2 egg whites

2 teaspoons vanilla extract

1/3 cup chopped pecans

3/4 cup skim milk

1 (4-serving) instant chocolate fudge pudding and pie filling mix

1 (8-ounce) container fat-free frozen whipped topping, thawed, divided

1/2 teaspoon almond extract

Chocolate shavings for decoration, if desired

1. Preheat oven 350°F. Coat 9-inch pie plate with nonstick cooking spray.

2. In small cup, stir together water and 1 teaspoon coffee until dissolved.

3. In large bowl, combine brownie mix, coffee mixture, egg, egg whites, and vanilla, stirring until well mixed. Add pecans. Pour batter into prepared pie plate. Bake 25-28 minutes, or until set, don't overbake for fudgy center. Cool.

4. In large bowl, stir together milk and remaining 1/2 teaspoon instant coffee until coffee is dissolved. Whisk in pudding mix until thickened. Carefully fold in half of whipped topping.

5. Spread pudding mixture evenly over the cooled brownie pie. Add almond extract to remaining whipped topping and spread over pudding mixture. Refrigerate until serving. Top with chocolate shavings, if desired.

Nutritional information per serving:

Calories 367
Calories from fat 25%
Fat 10g
Saturated Fat 2g
Cholesterol 22mg
Sodium 338mg
Carbohydrate 62g
Dietary Fiber 1g
Sugars 38g
Protein 5g
Dietary Exchanges:
4 other carbohydrate, 2 fat

Spicy Advice

Look for instant dark roast or instant espresso coffee in the coffee section. Coffee may be omitted, if desired for a plain chocolate pie.

Chocolate Fudgies

Medium-Dark
Roast

**Nutritional information
per serving:**

Calories 58

Calories from fat 16%

Fat 1g

Saturated Fat 0g

Cholesterol 4mg

Sodium 98mg

Carbohydrate 11g

Dietary Fiber 0g

Sugars 6g

Protein 1g

Dietary Exchanges:
1/2 other carbohydrate

These melt in your mouth chocolate fudgy cookies made with basically three ingredients create a terrific easy-to-make simple surprise. For my loaded variation add 1/2 cup dark chocolate chips and 1/2 cup pecans.

Makes about 48 cookies

1 (18.25-ounce) box Devil's
   Food cake mix

1 egg

1 (8-ounce) container fat-free frozen
   whipped topping, thawed

1/4 cup confectioners sugar

1. Preheat oven 350°F. Coat baking sheet with nonstick cooking spray.

2. In bowl, mix together cake mix, egg, and whipped topping by hand. Batter will be sticky.

3. Spread confectioners sugar on plate. Form dough into teaspoon size balls and roll in confectioners sugar. Place on prepared pan. Bake 10-12 minutes.

Fudgy Brownie Pie

Peanutty Chocolate Crustless Pie

Medium-Light Roast

**Nutritional information
per serving:**

Calories 282
Calories from fat 50%
Fat 17g
Saturated Fat 5g
Cholesterol 42mg
Sodium 86mg
Carbohydrate 28g
Dietary Fiber 2g
Sugars 24g
Protein 9g
Dietary Exchanges:
2 other carbohydrate,
1 lean meat, 3 fat

So easy, no mixer needed! You'll enjoy this dynamic pie with a peanut butter filling laced with semi-sweet chocolate.

Makes 8-10 servings

2/3 cup sugar

2 eggs

2 egg whites

1 tablespoon vanilla extract

1/2 cup peanut butter

1/2 cup chopped peanuts

2/3 cup mini semi-sweet chocolate chips

1. Preheat oven 350°F. Coat 9-inch pie plate with nonstick cooking spray.

2. In mixing bowl, whisk together sugar, eggs, egg whites, vanilla, and peanut butter. Stir in peanuts and chocolate chips. Transfer to prepared plate. Bake 40-45 minutes or until pie is set.

Easy Chocolate Truffles Dipped in White Chocolate

Dark Roast

**Nutritional information
per serving:**

Calories 76
Calories from fat 47%
Fat 4g
Saturated Fat 2g
Cholesterol 3mg
Sodium 70mg
Carbohydrate 9g
Dietary Fiber 0g
Sugars 6g
Protein 1g
Dietary Exchanges:
1/2 other carbohydrate, 1 fat

Close your eyes for this bite of ecstasy—only three ingredients using your favorite familiar chocolate cookie. Make ahead and enjoy this rich and satisfying treat.

Makes 4 1/2 dozen truffles

1 (1 pound 2-ounce) package chocolate sandwich cookies

1 (8-ounce) package reduced-fat cream cheese

1 cup white chocolate chips

1. In food processor, combine chocolate sandwich cookies and cream cheese, pulsing until mixture forms a ball. Shape mixture into 1-inch balls and place on baking sheet lined with wax paper. Refrigerate 1 hour.

2. In microwave-safe dish, microwave white chocolate chips for one minute, remove and stir until melted and creamy. Dip top of each ball in white chocolate and return to wax paper. Refrigerate until white chocolate hardens.

Spicy Advice

Once truffles are hardened, can transfer to resealable plastic bag. Keep refrigerated.

Easy Chocolate Truffles Dipped in White Chocolate

I don't even butter my bread;
I consider that cooking.

Table for Two

You don't marry someone you can live with — *you marry the person who you cannot live without.*

Good Morning Cheese Grits

Medium-Dark Roast

Here's a quick all-in-one hearty morning meal. If using as a side, serves four.

Makes 2 (1-cup) servings

1/3 cup diced Canadian bacon
   or diced ham

1/2 cup quick grits

2 cups skim milk

1/2 cup fat-free chicken broth or milk

1/3 cup shredded reduced-fat sharp
   Cheddar cheese

1/2 teaspoon paprika

Dash cayenne pepper

1/4 cup chopped green onions

Salt and pepper to taste

1 In nonstick pot coated with nonstick cooking spray, cook Canadian bacon until begins to brown. Add grits, milk, and broth. Bring to boil, reduce heat, cover, and continue cooking until grits are done, about 5-7 minutes.

2 Stir in cheese, paprika, cayenne and green onions. Season to taste.

Nutritional information per serving:

Calories 316
Calories from fat 14%
Fat 5g
Saturated Fat 3g
Cholesterol 27mg
Sodium 614mg
Carbohydrate 45g
Dietary Fiber 2g
Sugars 13g
Protein 22g
Dietary Exchanges:
2 starch, 1 fat free milk,
1 1/2 lean meat

Spicy Advice

For a southern classic, add 1/2 pound cooked shrimp.

Quick Artichoke Soup

Five ingredients for an instant rich and creamy healthier soup success.

Makes 2 servings

1 (14-ounce) cans artichoke hearts,
   drained

1 (10 3/4-ounce) can 98% fat-free
   cream of mushroom soup

1/3 cup skim milk

2/3 cup fat-free chicken broth

2 tablespoons white wine or
   cooking wine

Dash cayenne pepper

1 In food processor, process artichokes until smooth. Add mushroom soup, milk, broth, wine, and cayenne. Blend until well combined.

2 Transfer to pot, warm over low heat or heat in microwave. Serve.

Nutritional information per serving:

Calories 161
Calories from fat 22%
Fat 4g
Saturated Fat 1g
Cholesterol 7mg
Sodium 1625mg
Carbohydrate 23g
Dietary Fiber 3g
Sugars 5g
Protein 6g
Dietary Exchanges:
1 starch, 2 vegetable,
1/2 fat

Potato Soup

This snazzy soup starts with hash browns, so no time-consuming potato peeling; almost faster than opening a can. I top with cheese and green onions.

Makes 2 (1-cup) servings

2 cups frozen hash brown potatoes, partially thawed

1 (14 1/2-ounce) can fat-free chicken broth

1/3 cup finely chopped onion

1 tablespoon all-purpose flour

1/3 cup skim milk

1 In medium nonstick pot, heat hash browns, broth, and onion to a boil, reduce heat, and cook, covered, about 8-10 minutes.

2 In small bowl, whisk together flour with milk. Add to potato mixture and bring to boil. Reduce heat, and cook, stirring, for 5 minutes or until thickened. For thinner soup, add more milk.

Serve with salad and/or sandwich for a meal pleaser. Substitute vegetable broth for vegetarian version.

Potato Soup

Barbecue Chicken Quesadillas

Medium-Light Roast

Nutritional information per serving:

Calories 477
Calories from fat 13%
Fat 6g
Saturated Fat 2g
Cholesterol 69mg
Sodium 1052mg
Carbohydrate 66g
Dietary Fiber 5g
Sugars 15g
Protein 34g
Dietary Exchanges:
3 starch, 1 1/2 other carbohydrate,
3 1/2 very lean meat

Spruce up leftover chicken into a light, quick evening meal or fun appetizer. Serve with salsa, avocado and/or sour cream.

Makes 2 tortillas

1/3 cup chopped red onion

1/2 teaspoon minced garlic

1 cup packed baby spinach

1 cup shredded cooked skinless chicken breast

1/4 cup barbecue sauce

4 (8-inch) flour tortillas

1/4 cup shredded part skim mozzarella cheese

1. In small nonstick skillet coated with nonstick cooking spray, sauté onion and garlic until almost tender, about 5 minutes. Add spinach, stirring until wilted.

2. In small bowl, combine chicken and barbecue sauce. Lay two tortillas flat and divide evenly with spinach mixture, chicken with sauce, and cheese. Top each with remaining tortilla.

3. In nonstick skillet coated with nonstick cooking spray, heat skillet and cook tortillas until light brown, several minutes, turn and cook on other side, until light brown and cheese is melted. Cut into fourths and serve.

My doctor told me to stop having intimate dinners for two; *unless there is another person.*

Beef Lettuce Wraps

Looking for a light dinner with substance—you will enjoy this stream-lined version of a favorite Asian wrap. Look for shredded carrots in a bag.

Makes 2 (1-cup) servings

1/2 pound ground sirloin

2 tablespoons hoisin sauce

1 1/2 teaspoon low sodium soy sauce

1/2 teaspoon minced garlic

Salt and pepper to taste

1/4 cup shredded carrot

1/3 cup chopped water chestnuts

1/4 cup chopped green onions

2 tablespoons chopped peanuts

1 teaspoon sesame oil, optional

Boston lettuce leaves or red tip lettuce

1. In large nonstick skillet, cook meat over medium heat about 5-7 minutes, or until done. Drain excess fat. Remove from heat.

2. Stir in hoisin sauce, soy sauce, garlic and season to taste, mixing well. Add carrot, water chestnuts, green onions, peanuts and sesame oil, if desired. Spoon mixture onto a lettuce leaf and wrap. Repeat with remaining leaves.

Spicy Advice

Toss in shredded cabbage, cucumber, bean sprouts and serve with extra hoisin sauce-use whatever you have on hand or prefer.

Beef Lettuce Wraps

Taco Salad

Nutritional information per serving:

Calories 419
Calories from fat 21%
Fat 10g
Saturated Fat 4g
Cholesterol 74mg
Sodium 307mg
Carbohydrate 47g
Dietary Fiber 5g
Sugars 7g
Protein 35g
Dietary Exchanges:
2 1/2 starch, 2 vegetable,
3 1/2 lean meat

A couple pleaser, as this entrée salad is hearty enough to satisfy, and light enough to enjoy, making everyone content with a salad supper.

Makes 2 servings

1/2 pound ground sirloin

1/4 cup finely chopped onion

1/4 teaspoon minced garlic

1/4 teaspoon ground cumin

1 1/2 cups cooked rice (brown)

Salt and pepper to taste

2 cups mixed greens

1 tomato, chopped

1/4 cup shredded reduced-fat Cheddar cheese

1/4 cup chopped red onion

3 tablespoons nonfat sour cream or plain yogurt

3 tablespoons salsa

Low-fat tortilla chips (optional)

Spicy Advice

For leanest cuts of meat, look for those ending in 'loin' or 'round'.

1. In small nonstick skillet, cook meat, onion, and garlic until done, 5-7 minutes. Drain excess fat. Add cumin, rice and season to taste. Remove from heat, cool.

2. In bowl, combine mixed greens, tomato, cheese, red onion, and rice mixture.

3. In another bowl, mix sour cream and salsa. Toss with lettuce-rice mixture. Serve immediately, with extra salsa and chips, if desired.

Taco Salad

Fast Fish

Nutritional information per serving:

Calories 193
Calories from fat 36%
Fat 8g
Saturated Fat 1g
Cholesterol 43mg
Sodium 63mg
Carbohydrate 7g
Dietary Fiber 0g
Sugars 0g
Protein 19g
Dietary Exchanges:
1/2 starch, 3 lean meat

Looking for an easy way to cook the catch of the day or whatever available fish-effortless and excellent with a light lemon-garlic sauce. I add jalapenos for that extra punch!

Makes 2 servings

2 (4-6 ounce) fish fillets
Salt and pepper to taste
2 tablespoons all-purpose flour
1 tablespoon olive oil
1/2 teaspoon minced garlic

1 tablespoon lemon juice
1/4 cup white wine or cooking wine
1 tablespoon chopped jarred jalapenos, optional

1. Preheat oven 350°F. Coat small baking dish with nonstick cooking spray.

2. Season fish and coat with flour. In prepared baking dish, add olive oil and garlic; lay fish on top. Sprinkle fish with lemon juice, wine and jalapenos, if desired. Bake 20-25 minutes or until fish is flaky and done.

Easy Roasted Salmon ❄

Nutritional information per serving:

Calories 252
Calories from fat 25%
Fat 7g
Saturated Fat 1g
Cholesterol 97mg
Sodium 153mg
Carbohydrate 9g
Dietary Fiber 1g
Sugars 7g
Protein 37g
Dietary Exchanges:
1/2 other carbohydrate,
5 lean meat

Love salmon or never cooked it? You must try this incredible recipe--season salmon, pop in the oven and you have a terrific meal ready in minutes.

Makes 2 servings

1 tablespoon light brown sugar
2 teaspoons chili powder
1/2 teaspoon ground cumin

1/8 teaspoon ground cinnamon
Salt and pepper to taste
2 (6-ounce) salmon fillets

1. Preheat oven 400° F. Line baking sheet with foil.

2. In resealable plastic bag, mix together brown sugar, chili powder, cumin, cinnamon, and season to taste. Add salmon, coating all over and pat in seasoning.

3. Transfer to prepared pan. Bake 12-15 minutes or until fish flakes easily.

Ahi Tuna Tacos with Wasabi Cream and Mango Avocado Salsa

Nutritional information per serving (taco and wasabi cream only):

Calories 445
Calories from fat 10%
Fat 5g
Saturated Fat 1g
Cholesterol 65mg
Sodium 921mg
Carbohydrate 53g
Dietary Fiber 4g
Sugars 4g
Protein 44g
Dietary Exchanges:
3 1/2 starch,
5 very lean meat

Tuna is fast cooking with fast preparation and combined with fiery Wasabi Cream and fresh salsa, you have a marvelous meal in minutes. Here's a recipe for Mango Avocado Salsa, but any fruit salsa would be great to contrast the Wasabi Cream.

Makes two (2 taco) servings

1 teaspoon olive oil

10-12 ounces ahi tuna (1-inch thick)

2 teaspoons taco seasoning mix

4 (8-inch) flour tortillas

Wasabi Cream (recipe follows)

Avocado Mango Salsa (recipe follows)

1. In nonstick pan, heat olive oil until hot. Season tuna on both sides with taco seasoning and add to pan. Sear 1 minute per side or until tuna is cooked on the outside, but rare inside. Set aside.

2. Cover tortillas with damp paper towel and microwave 30 seconds. Fill tortillas with tuna, top with Wasabi Cream (see recipe) and Mango Avocado Salsa or salsa of choice.

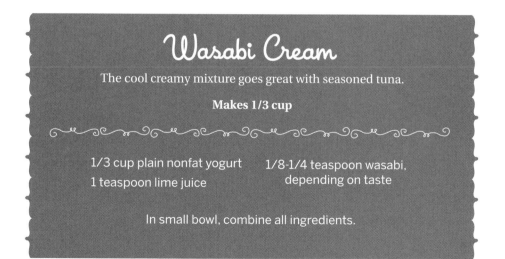

Wasabi Cream

The cool creamy mixture goes great with seasoned tuna.

Makes 1/3 cup

1/3 cup plain nonfat yogurt
1 teaspoon lime juice

1/8-1/4 teaspoon wasabi, depending on taste

In small bowl, combine all ingredients.

Mango Avocado Salsa

This fruity salsa with sweet mango, mild avocado and spicy jalapenos makes the ultimate complement to tuna tacos.

Makes 1 cup

1/3 cup chopped avocado

1/2 cup chopped mango

2 tablespoons chopped
red onion

1 teaspoon chopped
jarred jalapeno

1 tablespoon lime juice

In small bowl, combine all ingredients.

Ahi Tuna Tacos with Wasabi Cream
and Mango Avocado Salsa

Shrimp and Artichoke Dijon

Medium-Dark Roast

Delicious dinner in a flash with shrimp and artichokes in a creamy Dijon sauce.

Makes 2 servings

1 tablespoon olive oil

1/2 teaspoon minced garlic

2 teaspoons all-purpose flour

1/4 cup fat-free chicken broth

2 tablespoons white wine or cooking wine, optional

1/2 pound medium large shrimp, peeled

1 (5-ounce) can fat-free evaporated milk

1 tablespoon Dijon mustard

Salt and pepper to taste

1/2 cup quartered artichokes

2 tablespoons chopped parsley

1 In large nonstick skillet coated with nonstick cooking spray, heat oil and add garlic, stir quickly. Add flour, stirring 30 seconds and gradually add broth and wine, stirring, over medium heat, until thickened, about 2 minutes. Add shrimp.

2 Gradually add milk, mustard, and season to taste. Bring to boil, reduce heat and cook shrimp until done, about 4-5 minutes. Add artichokes and parsley. Serve.

Spicy Advice

Serve with yellow rice tossed with green onion stems.

Shrimp and Artichoke Dijon

Seared Scallops wrapped in Prosciutto

Nutritional information per serving:

Calories 169
Calories from fat 27%
Fat 5g
Saturated Fat 2g
Cholesterol 62mg
Sodium 690mg
Carbohydrate 4g
Dietary Fiber 0g
Sugars 1g
Protein 26g
Dietary Exchanges:
4 lean meat

Two ingredients and you appear as a gourmet chef. This versatile recipe makes a great entrée, appetizer, hot or even cold! To cook crisp scallops, make sure scallops are very dry and don't touch in pan.

Makes 2 servings

1/2 pound sea scallops
2 ounces prosciutto slices

1. Thaw, rinse and drain scallops; drying well in paper towel. Wrap prosciutto in narrow strips around each scallop. Secure with toothpick. Can refrigerate until ready to cook.

2. In large nonstick skillet coated with nonstick cooking spray, add dry scallops to hot pan, making sure edges don't touch each other. Cook 3-4 minutes, until golden brown, and turn to cook on other side about 2 minutes or until crisp and done, soft to touch and flake with fork.

Chicken Pesto Personal Pizza ❄

Nutritional information per serving:

Calories 354
Calories from fat 27%
Fat 11g
Saturated Fat 4g
Cholesterol 58mg
Sodium 661mg
Carbohydrate 37g
Dietary Fiber 6g
Sugars 2g
Protein 29g
Dietary Exchanges:
2 1/2 starch, 3 lean meat

Short on time but want a terrific meal? Go Mediterranean with pizza. Look for pre-made pesto in the grocery.

Makes 2 pizzas

2 whole wheat pitas
2 teaspoons pesto
6 tablespoons shredded part-skim mozzarella cheese
2/3 cup shredded cooked or grilled chicken

2 tablespoons chopped artichoke hearts
2 tablespoons chopped sun-dried tomatoes (reconstituted in hot water)
2 tablespoons crumbled reduced-fat feta cheese

1. Preheat oven 350°F. Coat baking pan with nonstick cooking spray.

2. Cover pitas with pesto and layer with remaining ingredients. Place on prepared pan and bake 10-12 minutes or until cheese is melted and pita is crisp.

Chicken and Sausage Jiffy Jambalaya

Dark Roast

Leftover cooked chicken turns magically into another easy southern favorite. Serve over rice.

Makes 2 servings

4 ounces reduced-fat smoked sausage, diced

1/2 pound cooked boneless, skinless chicken breasts, cut in strips or chunks

1 1/4 cups salsa

1/2 teaspoon dried thyme leaves

1/2 cup chopped green onions

1. In large nonstick skillet, cook sausage over medium heat until done. Drain any excess grease. Add chicken, salsa, and thyme. Bring to a boil, reduce heat, and add green onions, cooking 5 minutes longer. Serve over rice.

Spicy Advice

Pick up frozen pre-cooked, grilled sliced chicken breast fillets for grilled flavor.

Chicken and Sausage Jiffy Jambalaya

Terrific Tuscan Chicken ❄

Who says two people can't have a power-packed mouth-watering dinner? This quick chicken dish goes great with pasta.

Makes 2 servings

2 (6-ounce) boneless, skinless chicken breasts

Salt and pepper to taste

2 tablespoons olive oil

1/2 cup chopped onion

2 Roma tomatoes, chopped

1 teaspoon minced garlic

1 tablespoon capers, drained

2 tablespoons sliced black or Kalamata olives

1/2 (14-ounce) can artichoke heart quarters, drained

1/3 cup white wine or cooking wine

2 cups baby spinach

Grated Parmesan cheese, optional

If a recipe calls for fresh chopped tomatoes, canned chopped tomatoes, drained, may be substituted.

1. Between two sheets of plastic wrap or wax paper, pound each chicken breast until about 1/4-inch thick. Season to taste.

2. In large nonstick skillet coated with nonstick cooking spray, cook chicken breasts on both sides until done, about 5-7 minutes. Remove from skillet to serving platter.

3. In same nonstick skillet, heat olive oil and cook onion until tender, about 5 minutes. Add tomatoes, garlic, capers, olives, and artichokes, and cook until tomatoes are soft, about 5 minutes.

4. Add wine, stirring, and cook until well heated. Add spinach, cooking until wilted. Return chicken to skillet and sprinkle with Parmesan cheese, if desired.

I love to cook with wine... **Sometimes, I even add it to the food.**

Lemon Chicken with Pistachios

**Nutritional information
per serving:**

Calories 323
Calories from fat 35%
Fat 12g
Saturated Fat 2g
Cholesterol 99mg
Sodium 112mg
Carbohydrate 9g
Dietary Fiber 1g
Sugars 1g
Protein 42g
Dietary Exchanges:
1/2 starch, 5 lean meat

Time troubles? This chic recipe with lemon and pistachios has flair.

Makes 2 servings

2 (6-ounce) boneless, skinless
  chicken breasts

2 tablespoons all-purpose flour

Salt and pepper to taste

1 tablespoon olive oil

2 tablespoons lemon juice

2 tablespoons chopped
  pistachios, toasted

1. Lightly dredge chicken in flour seasoned to taste. Shake off excess flour.

2. In large nonstick skillet, heat olive oil and lemon juice. Add chicken and cook 10-15 minutes, or until chicken is done. Remove chicken to platter.

3. Add nuts to pan drippings and heat through, scraping pan to get every last drop sauce. Spoon nut mixture over chicken and serve.

Lamb Choppers Delish

Dark Roast

**Nutritional information
per serving:**

Calories 355
Calories from fat 35%
Fat 14g
Saturated Fat 5g
Cholesterol 121mg
Sodium 522mg
Carbohydrate 16g
Dietary Fiber 1g
Sugars 10g
Protein 40g
Dietary Exchanges:
1 other carbohydrate,
5 lean meat

Give lamb a try. Simple preparation with few ingredients, and bundles of flavor.

Makes 2 servings

1 1/3 pounds lamb loin chops
  (approximately 4)

Garlic powder to taste

Salt and pepper to taste

2 tablespoons Dijon mustard

1 tablespoon honey

2 tablespoons Italian or seasoned
  bread crumbs

1. Preheat broiler. Cover baking sheet with foil.

2. Season both sides of lamb chops with garlic powder, salt and pepper. Place on prepared pan. In small bowl, mix together mustard and honey; spread over lamb chops. Sprinkle with bread crumbs.

3. Place lamb chops under broiler and broil 8-10 minutes, depending on how you like them cooked. Watch carefully-not too close to broiler!

Sirloin Strips with Marsala Sauce ❄

This combination of sirloin, portabellas and Marsala turns simple ingredients into an extraordinary meal. Serve with rice or pasta to take advantage of the wonderful sauce.

Makes 2 servings

1/2-3/4 pound sirloin steak, trimmed and cut into 3/4 inch strips

2 teaspoons olive oil

1/2 cup chopped onion

1 cup sliced baby portabella mushrooms

1 teaspoon minced garlic

2 tablespoons all-purpose flour

1 cup beef broth

2 tablespoons Marsala wine or cooking wine

1/2 teaspoon dried thyme leaves

Salt and pepper to taste

Chopped green onions, garnish

1 In large nonstick skillet coated with nonstick cooking spray, brown steak over medium heat, stirring about 5-7 minutes. Remove from pan, set aside.

2 In same skillet, add olive oil and cook onion, mushrooms and garlic until tender, 5-7 minutes. Sprinkle with flour, stirring 30 seconds.

3 Gradually add broth, stirring constantly. Bring to boil, cooking several minutes until thickened. Add Marsala and thyme. Season to taste.

4 Return to boil and add steak to pan, continue cooking until done. Serve with chopped green onions.

Creamed Corn

Nutritional information per serving:

Calories 198
Calories from fat 28%
Fat 7g
Saturated Fat 4g
Cholesterol 16mg
Sodium 65mg
Carbohydrate 34g
Dietary Fiber 4g
Sugars 8g
Protein 6g
Dietary Exchanges:
2 1/2 starch, 1 fat

Sometimes I use fresh corn on the cob and sometimes I grab frozen corn from my freezer, either way, this simple side goes well with any entrée.

Makes 2 (1/2 cup) servings

1 tablespoon butter

1/4 cup chopped onion

1 1/2 cups corn

1 teaspoon all-purpose flour

1/3 cup skim milk

Pinch sugar

Salt and pepper to taste

1. In small nonstick skillet, melt butter and sauté onion 3 minutes. Add corn, and continue to cook 5 minutes longer, stirring.

2. Sprinkle with flour and stir one minute. Add milk and sugar. Bring to boil, lower heat, and continue cooking until thickened. Season to taste. Add more milk if needed.

Creamed Corn

Roasted Garlic Broccoli

Pop broccoli in the oven, while you prepare the rest of the dinner. Roasting broccoli is a simple way to intensify the natural flavor. Roasting is cooking at a high temperature that browns, caramelizes and crisps.

Makes 2 servings

4 cups broccoli florets

1 tablespoon olive oil

2 teaspoons minced garlic

Salt and pepper to taste

1. Preheat oven 450°F. Line baking sheet with foil.
2. Toss broccoli with olive oil and garlic on prepared pan. Roast 20 minutes, stirring after 10 minutes. Remove from oven and season to taste.

Angel Hair with Edamame

Make this simple yet special pasta for a jolt of crunch, flavor and nutrition.

Makes 2 servings

4 ounces angel hair (whole wheat pasta)

1/2 cup shelled edamame

1 tablespoon olive oil

1/2 teaspoon minced garlic

1 tablespoon finely chopped parsley

Salt and pepper to taste

1. Cook pasta according to package directions. Drain and set aside. Cook edamame in microwave according to package directions, set aside.
2. In large nonstick skillet, heat olive oil, and sauté garlic and parsley one minute. Add pasta and edamame, toss, season to taste.

Spicy Advice

Shelled edamame is found in freezer section of grocery-high in fiber, protein and nutrition.

Stuffed Greek Potatoes

Nutritional information per serving:

Calories 229
Calories from fat 13%
Fat 3g
Saturated Fat 1g
Cholesterol 4mg
Sodium 296mg
Carbohydrate 43g
Dietary Fiber 4g
Sugars 4g
Protein 8g
Dietary Exchanges:
3 starch

Make extra stuffed potatoes for your freezer to pull out for last minute meals.

Hearty vegetarian meal or super side full of Mediterranean flavors.

Makes 2 servings

2 medium baking potatoes

3 tablespoons nonfat plain yogurt

1 teaspoon dried oregano leaves

2 tablespoons chopped Kalamata olives

1/4 cup chopped green onions

2 tablespoons crumbled reduced-fat feta cheese

1. Preheat oven 400°F.

2. Wash potatoes and dry thoroughly. Place potatoes directly on oven rack, and bake approximately 1 hour or until soft when squeezed. Let potatoes cool to handle. Cut thin slice off top of each potato and scoop out inside, leaving thin shell.

3. In bowl, mash potatoes with yogurt and oregano until creamy. Stir in olives, green onions and feta. Spoon mixture into shells.

4. Reduce oven 350°F. Bake approximately 15 minutes or until cheese is melted and potatoes are hot, or can heat in microwave.

Stuffed Greek Potatoes

Banana Split Trifle

Medium-Dark Roast

Who turns down a banana split? This dessert is the height of indulgence. Can make individual servings.

Makes 4 servings (two for the next day)

1 (5-ounce) package sponge cake desserts cakes

1 (4-serving) package instant banana pudding and pie filling mix

1 1/2 cups skim milk

1 banana, sliced

1 cup sliced strawberries

2 tablespoons caramel topping

1 cup fat-free frozen whipped topping, thawed

1 Slice sponge cakes in half. In bowl, whisk pudding mix with milk until thick.

2 In glass bowl, layer half sponge cake slices, pudding, banana, strawberries, caramel topping, and whipped topping. Repeat layers, ending with whipped topping. Refrigerate until serving.

Spicy Advice

Angel food cake may be substituted for sponge cakes (usually found by strawberries) and chocolate topping may be used for caramel.

Lemon Sublime

Leave it to Pam to create a drink reminiscent of a favorite Italian spa to enjoy at home. Light with a bit of a kick!

Makes 2 servings

8 ounces champagne

1 cup lemon sherbet or sorbet

2 tablespoons vodka

Dash Chambord, optional

1 In blender, mix all ingredients, blend only until smooth (mixture should be liquefied enough to drink but still thick).

2 Pour into champagne glasses. If desired splash drop of Chambord on top of drink.

Frozen Banana and Cookie Dessert

Flavored Coffee

Nutritional information per serving:

Calories 348
Calories from fat 28%
Fat 11g
Saturated Fat 4g
Cholesterol 15mg
Sodium 129mg
Carbohydrate 52g
Dietary Fiber 2g
Sugars 31g
Protein 4g
Dietary Exchanges:
1 fruit, 2 1/2 other
carbohydrate, 2 fat

Four ingredients, bananas, whipped topping, cookies and coffee liqueur create this trouble-free, yet, awesome dessert.

Makes 2 servings

3 chocolate chunk cookies

2 tablespoons coffee liqueur

1 large banana, sliced

1/3 cup fat-free frozen whipped

topping, thawed

Cocoa or chocolate shavings

1. Quickly dip each cookie in shallow bowl with liqueur, break in large pieces. Place half of dipped cookies in bottom of two dessert dishes.

2. Layer with half banana slices in each dish and half whipped topping. Repeat layers ending with dollop of whipped topping. Refrigerate until serving. Sprinkle with cocoa, if desired.

This extraordinary dessert would be one to make for a crowd as it is make-ahead, delicious and refreshing. Just four times it or whatever amount servings you need—make in 9x9x2 inch pan and cut into servings.

Friendship is a wonderful
thing as it fills us with happiness
still leaving room for dessert!

Frozen Banana and Cookie Dessert

Food for the Mood

Great food is like great lovin'. The more you have the more you want.

Shrimp Dumplings with Asian Sauce ❄

Get your friend's attention with these easy dumplings bursting with flavor for a party in your mouth.

Makes 24 dumplings

1 cup medium peeled shrimp

1 cup packed baby spinach

3 tablespoons chopped water chestnuts

1 tablespoon sesame oil

2 teaspoons finely grated fresh ginger

1 teaspoon sherry

2 tablespoons finely chopped green onions

24 won ton wrappers

Asian Sauce (recipe follows)

Nutritional information per serving:

Calories 37
Calories from fat 19%
Fat 1g
Saturated Fat 0g
Cholesterol 11mg
Sodium 52mg
Carbohydrate 5g
Dietary Fiber 0g
Sugars 0g
Protein 2g
Dietary Exchanges: 1/2 starch

1. In nonstick skillet, cook shrimp until almost done, add spinach, continue cooking until shrimp are done and spinach wilted. Cool.

2. In food processor, pulse shrimp mixture until chopped. Add water chestnuts, sesame oil, ginger, and sherry, pulsing until mixture forms coarse paste. Add green onions.

3. Place 1 teaspoon shrimp mixture in center of each won ton square. Bring corners together over center of filling, pinch and twist to enclose creating a pouch.

4. In large nonstick skillet coated with nonstick cooking spray, bring small amount of water to boil (about 1/2-inch) in skillet, arrange dumplings, do not touch each other. Steam, covered, 8 minutes or until dumpling dough is done. Serve with Asian Sauce (see recipe).

Spicy Advice

Make ahead and refrigerate until cooking, or cook ahead and reheat in the microwave so the night is yours.

Asian Sauce

A blitz of Asian flavors that perfectly complements the dumplings.

Makes 1/4 cup

2 tablespoons low sodium soy sauce

2 tablespoons water

1/2 teaspoon sugar

1 tablespoon grated fresh ginger

Dash red pepper flakes or Asian chili sauce

1 green onion, finely chopped

In small bowl, combine all ingredients.

Margarita Shrimp

Medium-Dark Roast

All the margarita makings in this recipe will put you in the mood and the fiesta of flavors will insure fun. I like to serve with avocado slices as an appetizer.

Makes 4 servings

4 tablespoons orange liqueur, divided
3 tablespoons lime juice, divided
2 tablespoons tequila
2 tablespoons olive oil, divided
1/2 teaspoon minced garlic
1/2 fresh jalapeno pepper, seeded and minced
Salt to taste

2 tablespoons finely chopped fresh cilantro
1 1/2 pounds medium-large peeled shrimp
1 tablespoon all-purpose flour
3/4 cup fat-free chicken broth
Finely chopped cilantro, garnish

1. Combine 1 tablespoon orange liqueur, 1 tablespoon lime juice, tequila, 1 tablespoon olive oil, garlic, jalapeno pepper, salt and cilantro in resealable plastic bag; add shrimp. Refrigerate 1 hour.

2. In large nonstick skillet, add shrimp, discarding marinade and cook until shrimp are done, about 5-7 minutes. Remove from pan.

3. In same pan, add remaining 1 tablespoon oil, and add flour, stirring for one minute. Gradually add chicken broth, stirring, and bring to boil, cooking until thickened.

4. Stir in remaining 3 tablespoons orange liqueur and 2 tablespoons lime juice. Heat and return shrimp to pan. Serve. Sprinkle with cilantro, if desired.

Spicy Advice

Orange juice may be substituted for orange liqueur.

Fig, Caramelized Onion, Prosciutto & Goat Cheese Pizza ❄

Figs, considered a symbol of fertility and revered as an aphrodisiac, turn pizza into an alluring palate pleasing masterpiece.

Makes 8 servings

1 teaspoon plus 1 tablespoon olive oil, divided

1 small onion, thinly sliced

Pinch of sugar

1 (12-ounce) thin pizza crust

2 tablespoons orange marmalade

4 ounces figs, sliced in thirds

2 ounces prosciutto, cut into pieces

1/2 cup crumbled goat cheese

1/4 cup shredded part-skim mozzarella cheese

1 teaspoon dried rosemary leaves, optional

1. In small nonstick skillet, heat 1 teaspoon olive oil and sauté onion, stirring occasionally, about 10 minutes until start to turn golden. Add sugar and continue cooking until caramel color. Set aside to cool.

2. Preheat oven 450°F. On pizza crust, spread remaining 1 tablespoon olive oil and cover with orange marmalade. Arrange cooled onions, figs, prosciutto, goat cheese and mozzarella on crust.

3. Sprinkle with rosemary, if desired. Bake 10-15 minutes or until cheese is melted and crust crisp.

Figs are high in fiber and potassium. Can't find figs, just substitute dates.

Beer Bread

Say the word beer and you have your man's attention and when he smells the aroma of homemade bread, the evening is yours.

Makes 16 servings

4 cups self-rising flour

1/4 cup sugar

1 (16-ounce) bottle light beer

2 tablespoons butter, melted

1. Preheat oven 400°F. Coat 9x 5x 3-inch loaf pan with nonstick cooking spray

2. In large bowl, mix together flour, sugar, and beer, mixing only until moistened.

3. Transfer batter into prepared pan. Bake 50 minutes or until golden brown. Remove from oven, pour melted butter over top.

French Onion Soup ❄

Start your evening off special. Sophisticated presentation with simple preparation.

Makes 8 (1-cup) servings

1 tablespoon olive oil

6 cups thinly sliced onions

1/2 pound sliced baby portabellas

1 teaspoon sugar

4 cloves garlic, peeled and sliced

1/4 cup sherry

1 tablespoon Dijon mustard

1/2 teaspoon dried thyme leaves

2 tablespoons all-purpose flour

6 cups beef broth

1 cup white wine or cooking wine

Salt and pepper to taste

8 (1/2-inch thick) slices French bread, toasted

1 cup shredded part-skim mozzarella cheese

1/2 cup grated Parmesan cheese

The baby portabellas give the soup a rich earthy flavor.

1. In large nonstick pot, heat olive oil and sauté onions and portabellas on medium heat, stirring, until onions are golden and very soft, about 10-15 minutes. Add sugar and garlic; continue cooking 15-20 minutes more, stirring. Add sherry, stirring to loosen any brown bits from pot.

2. Add mustard, thyme, and flour, and stir one minute. Add broth and wine. Bring to boil, reduce heat, and cook about 20-30 minutes longer. Season to taste.

3. In bowl, ladle hot soup, top with bread and sprinkle with mozzarella and Parmesan cheese. Microwave or broil (oven-proof bowl) until cheese melts. Serve.

French Onion Soup

Italian Wedding Soup

Nutritional information per serving:

Calories 153
Calories from fat 19%
Fat 3g
Saturated Fat 1g
Cholesterol 40mg
Sodium 433mg
Carbohydrate 17g
Dietary Fiber 2g
Sugars 2g
Protein 14g
Dietary Exchanges:
1 starch, 1 1/2 lean meat

Need to hint to your honey about the big day, or looking for a calming comfort food? Think of this as a first-rate chicken soup with mini-meatballs and loads of flavor.

Makes 12 (1-cup) servings with 3-4 mini meatballs

1 cup chopped onion

1/2 cup chopped celery

1 cup diced carrots

1 tablespoon minced garlic

8 cups fat-free chicken broth

1 1/2 cups beef broth

1 teaspoon dried oregano leaves

1 cup orzo pasta

Mini Meatballs (recipe follows)

6 cups fresh baby spinach

Salt and pepper to taste

1. In large nonstick pot coated with nonstick cooking spray, sauté onion, celery, carrots and garlic until tender, 7 minutes. Add both broths and oregano.

2. Add orzo. Bring to boil, reduce heat, and cook 5 minutes. Add Mini Meatballs (see recipe), and continue cooking 8 minutes or until meatballs are done. Add spinach, cooking a few more minutes until wilted. Season to taste.

Mini Meatballs

Wait until you try these meatballs!

1 pound ground sirloin

1 egg white

2 tablespoons chopped parsley

1 egg

1 teaspoon minced garlic

1/4 cup Italian bread crumbs

3 tablespoons grated Parmesan cheese

Salt and pepper to taste

Combine all ingredients into bowl and shape meat mixture into 1-inch diameter meatballs.

Oyster Artichoke Soup

Nutritional information per serving:

Calories 180
Calories from fat 30%
Fat 6g
Saturated Fat 1g
Cholesterol 30mg
Sodium 501mg
Carbohydrate 21g
Dietary Fiber 3g
Sugars 5g
Protein 10g
Dietary Exchanges:
1/2 starch, 2 vegetable,
1 lean meat, 1/2 fat

Oysters are high in zinc content, a mineral that aids in the production of testosterone and it was rumored that Casanova ate over 50 raw oysters a day to boost his libido. Even if you don't like raw oysters, you are sure to love this oyster, artichoke pairing in this simple seductive soup.

Makes 6 (1-cup) servings

2 tablespoons olive oil

1 bunch green onions, chopped

1 teaspoon minced garlic

1/4 cup all-purpose flour

1 1/2 cups fat-free chicken broth

1 pint oysters, reserving 1/2 cup oyster liquid

Dash cayenne

1/2 teaspoon dried thyme leaves

1 bay leaf

2 (14-ounce) cans artichoke hearts, drained and coarsely chopped

1/4 cup chopped parsley

1 cup fat-free half-and-half

1/4 cup sherry

1. In nonstick pot, heat olive oil and sauté green onions and garlic 5 minutes. Add flour, stirring constantly, gradually add chicken broth and reserved oyster liquid. Add cayenne, thyme and bay leaf.

2. Bring to boil, reduce heat, and cook about 15 minutes. Add oysters, artichokes and parsley, cooking until oysters curl around edges, 10 minutes.

3. Stir in half-and-half and sherry, cooking until thoroughly heated. Remove bay leaf before serving.

If freezing, may use chicken broth for oyster liquid, and add oysters when reheating to serve.

A good marriage is like a good wine,
it gets better with age.

Simple Salmon with Spinach Feta Stuffing

This magnificent dish is gourmet-on-the-go and takes minutes to prepare.

Makes 4 servings

2 ounces reduced-fat cream cheese

1/2 cup crumbled reduced-fat feta cheese

1/3 cup chopped red onion

1/2 cup chopped baby spinach

4 (6-ounce) salmon fillets

1. Preheat oven 350°F. Coat baking dish with nonstick cooking spray.

2. In bowl, combine cream cheese and feta with fork, mixing until blended. Add onion and spinach, combining well.

3. Split each piece of salmon in half lengthwise without cutting all the way through (make pocket). Divide filling in each fillet spreading to cover. Place top salmon piece back over filling and on prepared baking dish. Bake 20 minutes or until flaky and done.

Serve with Lemon Angel Hair Pasta with Pine Nuts, page 105.

Simple Salmon with Spinach Feta Stuffing

Stuffed Crab Poblano Peppers

Nutritional information per serving:

Calories 136
Calories from fat 37%
Fat 5g
Saturated Fat 3g
Cholesterol 63mg
Sodium 413mg
Carbohydrate 4g
Dietary Fiber 1g
Sugars 2g
Protein 17g
Dietary Exchanges:
2 1/2 lean meat

No fuss and super simple to make! Mild peppers stuffed with a creamy crab mixture wrapped with turkey bacon, give you the perfect balance of flavors. Remember, it is said "hot food" generates a physiological response as when you get excited, so spice things up in your kitchen!

Makes 8 pepper halves

1 (8-ounce) package reduced-fat cream cheese

1/3 cup chopped green onions

1/3 cup chopped red onions

1 teaspoon minced garlic

Salt and pepper to taste

1 pound lump or white crabmeat, picked for shells

4 Poblano peppers (about 3/4 pound), halved and seeded

8 slices turkey bacon

1. Preheat oven 375°F. Line baking sheet with foil.

2. In microwave-safe dish, microwave cream cheese 30 seconds or to just soften. Mix with green onions, red onions, garlic and season to taste. Carefully fold in crabmeat.

3. Stuff pepper halves with crab mixture, wrap each pepper with turkey bacon and place on prepared pan. Bake 35-40 minutes or until peppers are tender and bacon is done.

Canned crabmeat or cooked shrimp may be used.

You can tell how long a couple has been married by whether they are on their *first, second or third bottle of hot sauce.*

Wasabi Crab Cakes with Ginger Sauce

Nutritional information per serving:

Calories 153
Calories from fat 26%
Fat 4g
Saturated Fat 0g
Cholesterol 73mg
Sodium 470mg
Carbohydrate 13g
Dietary Fiber 1g
Sugars 1g
Protein 15g
Dietary Exchanges:
1 starch, 2 lean meat

Wasabi, a spicy 'SinSation', and soy sauce turn crab cakes into an Asian paradise and the Ginger Sauce knocks it out of the park. Make ahead, refrigerate and cook when ready to serve.

Makes 8 servings

1/2 cup chopped green onion

3 tablespoons light mayonnaise

1 egg

1 1/2 tablespoons wasabi paste (according to taste)

2 teaspoons seasoned rice vinegar

2 teaspoons low sodium soy sauce

1 teaspoon lemon juice

1 1/2 cups panko bread crumbs, divided

1 pound white or lump crabmeat, picked through for shells

Ginger Sauce (see below)

1. In bowl, combine green onion, mayonnaise, egg, wasabi, rice vinegar, soy sauce, and lemon juice. Fold in 1/2 cup panko crumbs and crabmeat.

2. Form crab mixture into 8 patties, pat remaining 1 cup panko crumbs onto both sides of patties. For best results, refrigerate at least 1 hour or up to 24 hours before cooking.

3. Heat nonstick skillet coated with nonstick cooking spray over medium heat and cook crab cakes 3–5 minutes on each side or until golden brown. Serve with Ginger Sauce (see recipe).

Ginger Sauce

Fresh ginger is a must for this remarkable sauce.
The ginger scent stimulates circulation.

Makes 1/2 cup

3 tablespoons light mayonnaise

3 tablespoons nonfat yogurt or sour cream

2 tablespoons grated fresh ginger

1 teaspoon seasoned rice vinegar

In small bowl, combine all ingredients.

Wasabi Crab Cakes with Ginger Sauce

Cooking is like love. You should feel free to express yourself or don't enter in to it at all.

Blackberry Chicken

The longer the chicken cooks in the sauce, the better it gets!

The sultry blend of blackberry jam and balsamic vinegar infuse the chicken with unbeatable flavors while the caramelized onions make a slightly sweet, savory sauce.

Makes 4 servings

1 teaspoon olive oil

1/2 cup chopped red onion

1 1/2 pounds boneless, skinless chicken breasts

1/2 teaspoon dried thyme leaves

Salt and pepper to taste

1 tablespoon all-purpose flour

1/2-3/4 cup fat-free chicken broth

1/2 cup seedless blackberry jam

2 tablespoons balsamic vinegar

1. In large nonstick skillet, heat olive oil and sauté onion 5 minutes. Season chicken with thyme and season to taste. Dust with flour.

2. Add chicken to pan, cooking until browned on each side, about 7-10 minutes. Add broth and continue cooking another 15 minutes.

3. Add jam and balsamic vinegar, bring to boil, reduce heat, and cook chicken for another 15-20 minutes or until tender.

Blackberry Chicken

Chicken with Wonderful Tomato Sauce

Nutritional information per serving:

Calories 286
Calories from fat 26%
Fat 8g
Saturated Fat 2g
Cholesterol 96mg
Sodium 528mg
Carbohydrate 9g
Dietary Fiber 1g
Sugars 4g
Protein 39g
Dietary Exchanges:
2 vegetable, 3 lean meat

Remember, you can dress up a plain bird with extras to make any 'dish' extraordinary. Tender chicken in this tasty tomato sauce turns special.

Makes 6 servings

2 pounds boneless, skinless chicken breasts
Salt and pepper to taste
3 tablespoons all-purpose flour
2 tablespoons olive oil
1 red bell pepper, cored and thinly sliced
1 yellow bell pepper, cored and thinly sliced
2 ounces prosciutto, chopped

1 teaspoon minced garlic
1 (14 1/2-ounce) can diced tomatoes with juice
1 cup fat-free chicken broth
1/2 cup white wine or cooking white wine
1 teaspoon dried thyme leaves
1 teaspoon dried oregano leaves

1. Season chicken with salt and pepper, lightly coat with flour.

2. In large nonstick skillet, heat olive oil over medium heat and brown chicken on both sides. Remove from pan, set aside.

3. In same pan, coated with nonstick cooking spray, add peppers and prosciutto, cook 5 minutes. Add garlic, continue cooking until peppers are tender.

4. Add tomatoes, broth, wine, thyme, and oregano scraping any brown bits from bottom of pan. Bring mixture to boil and return chicken to pan. Reduce heat and simmer, covered, until chicken is done, 25 - 30 minutes.

Spicy Advice

Serve with pasta or rice to take advantage of this fabulous sauce.

Oysters and Angel Hair

Turn oysters into a toss-together palate pleasing party with crispy oysters served over angel hair in a light garlic olive oil with tomatoes, sun-dried tomatoes, parsley and mushrooms. The Romans claimed oysters to be an aphrodisiac food; the verdict is up to you.

Makes 6 servings

12 ounces angel hair pasta

1 (16-ounce) container small oysters

1/3 cup Italian bread crumbs

2 tablespoons olive oil

1/2 pound sliced mushrooms

1 bunch green onions, chopped

2 teaspoons minced garlic

1/2 cup chopped fresh parsley

1/2 cup chopped tomatoes

Pinch sugar

1/3 cup chopped or sliced sun-dried tomatoes, reconstituted

3/4 cup fat-free chicken broth

Salt and pepper to taste

Grated Parmesan cheese, if desired

1. Cook pasta according to package directions. Drain and set aside. Drain oysters and toss bread crumbs and oysters together in a resealable plastic bag or bowl.

2. In large nonstick skillet coated with nonstick cooking spray, cook oysters over medium heat until browned. Remove to plate.

3. In same pan, heat olive oil and sauté mushrooms, green onions, garlic, and parsley, scraping bottom of pan to get bits, about 3 minutes. Add tomatoes and sugar, cooking until tender.

4. Add sun-dried tomatoes and broth, bring to boil, cook another 5 minutes. Toss pasta with tomato mixture. Season to taste. Serve pasta topped with oysters and sprinkle with Parmesan cheese, if desired.

Nutritional information per serving:

Calories 366
Calories from fat 19%
Fat 8g
Saturated Fat 1g
Cholesterol 40mg
Sodium 322mg
Carbohydrate 57g
Dietary Fiber 4g
Sugars 5g
Protein 16g
Dietary Exchanges:
3 1/2 starch, 1 vegetable,
3 lean meat

Spicy Advice

When a recipe calls for tomatoes, fresh or canned tomatoes, drained may be used.

Lemon Angel Hair Pasta with Pine Nuts

Pine nuts are considered to be an aphrodisiac so make this lover's lemon pasta side of choice with whatever you are serving!

Makes 4 servings

8 ounces angel hair pasta, reserving 1/4 cup cooking water

2 tablespoons olive oil

1 teaspoon minced garlic

2 tablespoons pine nuts, toasted

1/4 cup lemon juice

1 1/2 teaspoons grated lemon rind

1/4 cup chopped parsley

Salt and pepper to taste

1. Cook pasta according to package directions, reserving 1/4 cup cooking water; drain well and set aside.

2. In small nonstick skillet, heat olive oil and sauté garlic, stirring, one minute. Transfer to large bowl and add remaining ingredients, mixing well. Season to taste.

3. Add pasta with reserved cooking water to bowl and toss together until well combined. Serve warm or at room temperature.

Spicy Advice

I recommend using fresh lemons and parsley-but if not in the mood, hit the bottle (of lemon juice). Watch toasting pine nuts carefully as they burn very quickly!

← Lemon Angel Hair Pasta with Pine Nuts

Poppy Seed Pasta

Nutritional information per serving:

Calories 281
Calories from fat 23%
Fat 7g
Saturated Fat 2g
Cholesterol 8mg
Sodium 71mg
Carbohydrate 44g
Dietary Fiber 2g
Sugars 2g
Protein 9g
Dietary Exchanges:
3 starch, 1 fat

Had leftover pasta and decided to jazz it up with these few ingredients to round out a simple supper with an exceptional pasta side, ideal for a special someone.

Makes 4-6 servings

12 ounces bow tie pasta, reserving 1/2 cup cooking water

1 tablespoon olive oil

1 tablespoon butter

1 teaspoon minced garlic

1/3 cup finely chopped onion

2 tablespoons poppy seeds

3 tablespoons chopped parsley

1/4 cup grated Parmesan cheese

1. Cook pasta according to package directions, reserving 1/2 cup cooking water. Drain, and set aside.

2. In large nonstick skillet, heat olive oil and butter, and sauté garlic and onion 5 minutes. Add pasta, reserved pasta water, poppy seeds, parsley and Parmesan cheese, tossing well.

Poppy Seed Pasta

Vodka Pasta

Nutritional information per serving:

Calories 292
Calories from fat 20%
Fat 7g
Saturated Fat 1g
Cholesterol 8mg
Sodium 385mg
Carbohydrate 38g
Dietary Fiber 1g
Sugars 6g
Protein 11g
Dietary Exchanges:
2 1/2 starch, 1 vegetable,
1/2 very lean meat,1 fat

Exhilarating pasta? Alcohol lowers inhibitions and increases confidence making this a great choice to boost your kitchen confidence. Vodka sauce is basically a mild red sauce with Italian seasoning. Sprinkle with Parmesan cheese when serving, if desired.

Makes 4 - 6 servings

2 tablespoons olive oil

1 small onion, chopped

2 ounces chopped lean ham
   or prosciutto

1 teaspoon minced garlic

1 (14 1/2-ounce) can diced
   tomatoes and juice

1 1/2 teaspoons dried basil leaves

1 teaspoon dried oregano leaves

1/2 cup vodka

3/4 cup fat-free half-and-half

1/4 cup grated Parmesan cheese

8 ounces fettuccine

Salt and pepper to taste

1. In large nonstick skillet over medium heat, heat olive oil and sauté onion, ham and garlic 5 minutes, or until onion is tender.

2. Add tomatoes with juice, basil, oregano and vodka, simmering over low heat 10 minutes. Add half-and-half and Parmesan cheese, cooking until sauce slightly thickens, about 4 minutes.

3. Meanwhile, cook pasta according to package directions; drain. Toss fettuccine with tomato mixture, season to taste, serve immediately.

Spicy Advice

My daughter Haley added ground sirloin to turn it into a heartier main dish.

A woman accepted cooking as a chore
but man has made of it a recreation.

Margarita Cake

Medium-Dark Roast

Sweet and salty, light and refreshing, this white cake flavored with non-alcoholic margarita mix and lime, on a pretzel crust makes quite an "ole!"

Makes 24 servings

1 1/2 cups coarsely crushed pretzels

2 tablespoons light brown sugar

5 tablespoons butter, melted

1 (18.25-ounce) box white cake mix

1 1/4 cups bottled non-alcoholic margarita mix

1/4 cup canola oil

1 tablespoon grated lime rind

3 egg whites

1 (8-ounce) frozen fat-free whipped topping, thawed

Additional grated lime rind, if desired

1. Heat oven 350°F. Coat 13x9x2-inch pan with nonstick cooking spray.

2. In medium bowl, mix pretzels, brown sugar and melted butter. Press into pan.

3. In large bowl, beat cake mix, margarita mix, oil, lime rind and egg whites until well mixed. Carefully pour batter over pretzel mixture.

4. Bake 25-30 minutes or until light golden brown and top springs back when touched lightly in center. Cool completely. Frost with whipped topping; sprinkle with additional lime rind. Refrigerate.

Nutritional information per serving:

Calories 176

Calories from fat 34%

Fat 7g

Saturated Fat 2g

Cholesterol 6mg

Sodium 260mg

Carbohydrate 27g

Dietary Fiber 0g

Sugars 12g

Protein 2g

Dietary Exchanges:
2 other carbohydrate,
1 1/2 fat

Spicy Advice

Don't skip on the lime rind as it infuses mucho flavor essence in the cake.

Margarita Cake

White Chocolate Crème Brulee

Medium Roast

Fancy but have no fear as you can make this infamous dessert with my simple version- all the indulgence without the bulge! Romance in the air!

Makes 4 servings

1 (3-ounce) package instant white chocolate pudding and pie filling mix

1 1/2 cups skim milk

1/4 cup white crème de cocoa

6 teaspoons sugar

1. In bowl, whisk together pudding mix, milk and crème de cocoa. Pour into 4 small ramekins.

2. Refrigerate 5 -10 minutes or until set. Sprinkle each ramekin with 1 1/2 teaspoons sugar.

3. Preheat broiler. Broil, watching carefully, or use small 'chef's' torch to crystallize sugar. Serve.

White Chocolate Crème Brulee

Best Chocolate Peanut Clusters

Medium-Light Roast

Nutritional information per serving:

Calories 98
Calories from fat 59%
Fat 7g
Saturated Fat 3g
Cholesterol 0mg
Sodium 16mg
Carbohydrate 8g
Dietary Fiber 1g
Sugars 7g
Protein 3g
Dietary Exchanges:
1/2 other carbohydrate,
1 1/2 fat

Feeling sluggish after a long day--pop some chocolate as chocolate has a very pleasant mouth feel and contains obromine and caffeine, which are mood elevators.

Makes about 5 1/2 dozen

1 (12-ounce) bag dark chocolate chips
1 (4-ounce) bar German chocolate
8 ounces almond bark

2 cups dry roasted salted peanuts
1 1/2 cups unsalted dry roasted peanuts

1 In large nonstick pot, over low heat, melt chocolate, German chocolate and almond bark, stirring until melted. Stir in both peanuts. Let sit 10-15 minutes, stirring occasionally to cool and slightly thicken.

2 Drop by spoonfuls on baking sheet lined with wax paper and cool until hardens.

Best Chocolate Peanut Clusters

Caramel Pecan Candies

The romance of a box of enticing chocolates made easily and affordable.

Makes 30 candies

1 (14-ounce) package caramels, unwrapped

2 tablespoons skim milk

2 cups chopped pecans

1/2 cup dark chocolate chips or semi-sweet chocolate chips

1. In microwave-safe dish, combine caramels and milk in microwave 1 minute, stir, and microwave another minute or until melted. Stir in pecans, and drop by tablespoonful onto wax paper covered baking sheets. Let stand until firm.

2. Microwave chocolate in microwave-safe bowl 1 minute or until melted, stirring once.

3. Dip top of caramel candies into melted chocolate, allowing excess to drip; place on wax paper. Let get firm.

Nutritional information per serving:

Calories 120
Calories from fat 52%
Fat 7g
Saturated Fat 1g
Cholesterol 1mg
Sodium 33mg
Carbohydrate 14g
Dietary Fiber 1g
Sugars 11g
Protein 2g
Dietary Exchanges:
1 other carbohydrate,
1 1/2 fat

Hate unwrapping caramels-look for bag of caramel bits ready to use.

Caramel Pecan Candies

Effortless Entertaining

Dazzling Drinks

Piña Colada Brie

Nutritional information per serving:

Calories 176
Calories from fat 34%
Fat 7g
Saturated Fat 2g
Cholesterol 6mg
Sodium 260mg
Carbohydrate 27g
Dietary Fiber 0g
Sugars 12g
Protein 2g
Dietary Exchanges:
2 other carbohydrate,
1 1/2 fat

Did you know an easy way to cut brie is with dental floss?

Incredible!!! Think of velvety rich Brie paired with Piña Colada ingredients for a fabulous mouth-watering tropical paradise. Try serving with gingersnaps.

Makes 16-20 servings

1 (16-ounce) Brie

1 (8-ounce) can crushed pineapple, drained, divided

4 tablespoons light brown sugar, divided

3 tablespoons flaked coconut, divided

3 tablespoons chopped pecans

1. Preheat oven 325°F.

2. Carefully remove top rind of Brie, cut Brie in half. Place Brie bottom in oven-proof baking dish, cover with about two-thirds of pineapple, 2 tablespoons brown sugar and 1 tablespoon coconut.

3. Replace top and sprinkle with remaining 2 tablespoons brown sugar and pineapple. Bake 10-15 minutes or until brown sugar is melted.

4. Meanwhile, toast remaining 2 tablespoons coconut and pecans, careful not to burn. Sprinkle with toasted coconut and pecans. Serve.

Piña Colada Brie

Caponata

Nutritional information per serving:

Calories 29
Calories from fat 43%
Fat 1g
Saturated Fat 0g
Cholesterol 0mg
Sodium 111mg
Carbohydrate 4g
Dietary Fiber 1g
Sugars 2g
Protein 1g
Dietary Exchanges:
Free

When I tasted this dip, I asked my brother-in-law, Cannon, for his recipe, and he told me "it's yours from years ago!" I forgot about this delicious dip with the perfect harmony of textures and flavors. Make ahead, refrigerate, and best served at room temperature. Serve with Brushetta or pita chips.

Makes 48 (1/4-cup) servings

1/4 cup olive oil

2 medium unpeeled eggplants, cut into 1-inch cubes

2 onions, chopped

1 green pepper, cored and chopped

1 red bell pepper, cored and chopped

1 1/2 cups sliced celery

1 teaspoon minced garlic

1 (14-ounce) can diced fire-roasted tomatoes

1 (15-ounce) can tomato sauce

1/3 cup red wine vinegar

Salt and pepper to taste

2 tablespoons sugar

2 tablespoons dried basil leaves

1/2 cup chopped parsley

3/4 cup sliced stuffed green olives

1 In large nonstick pot, heat olive oil and sauté eggplant and onion until golden, about 5 minutes. Add remaining ingredients, stir gently.

2 Bring to boil, reduce heat, and cook, covered, 30 minutes, stirring occasionally. Remove lid and continue cooking about 10 minutes more, or until thickened. Serve at room temperature or refrigerate.

Spicy Advice

Caponata is a Sicilian dish usually composed of eggplant, onions, tomatoes, olives, capers and vinegar- served at room temperature. You can half this recipe.

I love the intense flavor of fire-roasted tomatoes but any canned tomatoes can be used.

Spinach Artichoke Dip

Quick and popular, my version with creamy Brie and Parmesan is hard to beat. Serve with chips or try red pepper squares and cucumber rounds.

Makes 20 (1/4-cup) servings

1 onion, chopped

1/3 cup all-purpose flour

2 cups skim milk

1 teaspoon minced garlic

2 (10-ounce) boxes frozen chopped spinach, thawed and drained

4 ounces Brie cheese, rind removed and cubed

1/3 cup grated Parmesan cheese

1 (14-ounce) can artichoke hearts, drained and quartered

Dash cayenne

Salt and pepper to taste

1. In nonstick pot coated with nonstick cooking spray, sauté onion until tender. Stir in flour. Gradually add milk, stirring constantly, heating until bubbly and thickened.

2. Add garlic, spinach, Brie, and Parmesan cheese, stirring until cheese is melted. Stir in artichokes, cayenne and season to taste.

Spicy Advice

Serve in an easy and impressive bread bowl. Cut thin slice off top of a round bread and scoop out soft inside bread, leaving a shell. Fill with spinach dip. Wrap tightly in foil and bake until hot, about 20-25 minutes. No clean up.

Spinach Artichoke Dip

Olive Cheese Cocktail Bread ❄️ 🥕

Freeze and please appetizer. Distinct flavors meld together for this outstanding party pick-up. Make ahead of time to pull out from freezer when desired.

Makes 48-50 miniature breads

1 bunch green onions, finely chopped

1/3 cup chopped Kalamata olives

1 (4-ounce) can chopped green chilies

1 (8-ounce) package shredded reduced-fat sharp Cheddar cheese

2 tablespoons olive oil

1 loaf cocktail rye bread or sourdough bread

1. In bowl, mix together all ingredients except bread. Spread on top bread slices.
2. Freeze flat on baking sheet few hours, place in resealable freezable plastic bags.
3. Preheat oven 350°F. Bake 10-12 minutes, until corners of bread start to turn brown.

Nutritional information per serving:

Calories 46
Calories from fat 36%
Fat 2g
Saturated Fat 1g
Cholesterol 2mg
Sodium 138mg
Carbohydrate 5g
Dietary Fiber 1g
Sugars 1g
Protein 2g
Dietary Exchanges: 1/2 starch

Spicy Advice

If cooking immediately, (not frozen) bake 8-10 minutes. Raid an olive bar for good quality Kalamata olives--makes a difference.

Black-Eyed Pea Dip ❄️

Open cans for a simple short-cut to this meaty black bean dip; hearty, healthy, and delicious. Ideal for New Year's Day but enjoyable year round.

Makes 24 (1/4-cup) servings

1/2 pound ground sirloin

1 onion, chopped

1 green or red bell pepper, cored and chopped

1 tablespoon all-purpose flour

1 tablespoon chopped jarred jalapenos

2 (15-ounce) cans black- eyed peas, rinsed and drained

1 (10-ounce) can diced tomatoes and green chilies

1 1/2 cups shredded reduced-fat Mexican blend cheese

1. In nonstick pot coated with nonstick cooking spray, cook meat, onion, and bell pepper, until meat is done.
2. Stir in flour, and add remaining ingredients, stirring until cheese is melted and dip heated thoroughly. Serve hot.

Nutritional information per serving:

Calories 66
Calories from fat 26%
Fat 2g
Saturated Fat 1g
Cholesterol 10mg
Sodium 222mg
Carbohydrate 7g
Dietary Fiber 1g
Sugars 1g
Protein 5g
Dietary Exchanges: 1/2 starch, 1/2 lean meat

Meaty Italian Dip ❄

Had friends over one day and they went wild over this recipe, a creamy hearty dip with robust Italian ingredients- had so many recipe requests and everyone ate more and more and more.

Makes 32 (1/4-cup) servings

1 pound ground sirloin

6 ounces ground breakfast turkey sausage

1/2 pound sliced mushrooms

1 cup chopped onion

1/2 cup minced roasted red peppers (found in jar)

1/2 cup sliced black olives

1 (14-ounce) can artichokes, drained and finely chopped

1 (14-ounce) can fire-roasted chopped tomatoes

2 teaspoons minced garlic

1 teaspoon dried basil leaves

1 teaspoon dried oregano leaves

1/2 cup grated Parmesan cheese

1 (8-ounce) package reduced-fat cream cheese

1/2 cup nonfat sour cream

1 In large nonstick pot, cook meat, sausage, mushrooms and onion until meat and sausage are done, about 5-7 minutes. Drain excess fat.

2 Add remaining ingredients, except sour cream and cook until cheese is melted and dip is well heated. Stir in sour cream, heat and serve.

Spicy Advice

Fire-roasted diced tomatoes have a roasted smoky flavor for a more intense tasting tomato.

Too much of a good thing is simply wonderful!

Eight Layered Greek Dip

Nutritional information per serving:

Calories 90
Calories from fat 58%
Fat 6g
Saturated Fat 0g
Cholesterol 1mg
Sodium 245mg
Carbohydrate 7g
Dietary Fiber 2g
Sugars 2g
Protein 2g
Dietary Exchanges:
1/2 starch, 1 fat

This is my go-to make-ahead recipe when I want an impressive knockout appetizer. Move over Mexican - this Mediterranean inspired dip will be your new party favorite-it is mine. Serve with pita chips.

Makes 10 servings

1 (10-ounce) container roasted red pepper hummus

1 cup coarsely chopped fresh baby spinach

1/2 cup chopped sun-dried tomatoes, reconstituted

1/2 cup chopped peeled cucumber

1/4 cup chopped red onion

1/4 cup crumbled reduced-fat feta cheese or crumbled goat cheese

2 tablespoons sliced Kalamata olives

1/4 cup chopped pecans, toasted

1. Spread hummus on 9-inch serving plate.

2. Sprinkle evenly with remaining ingredients, refrigerate until serving time.

Eight Layered Greek Dip

Fiesta Southwestern Cheesecake

Dark Roast

Make ahead and freeze this savory southwestern style cheesecake for an appetizer taste sensation. If freezing, top with salsa, when serving.

Makes 20 - 25 servings

Nutritional information per serving:

Calories 96
Calories from fat 58%
Fat 6g
Saturated Fat 4g
Cholesterol 26mg
Sodium 252mg
Carbohydrate 6g
Dietary Fiber 1g
Sugars 2g
Protein 4g
Dietary Exchanges:
1/2 other carbohydrate,
1/2 lean meat, 1 fat

1 cup toasted corn checks cereal crumbs

1 tablespoon butter, melted

1 tablespoon olive oil

2 (8-ounce) packages reduced-fat cream cheese

1/3 cup nonfat sour cream

1 egg

2 egg whites

1 teaspoon minced garlic

1/2 teaspoon chili powder

1/4 teaspoon ground cumin

1 cup shredded reduced-fat sharp Cheddar cheese

2 (4-ounce) cans chopped green chilies, drained

1 bunch green onions, chopped

1/2 cup chopped onion

2 cups salsa, divided

Spicy Advice

For extra flavor and kick, use a flavored salsa such as roasted tomato or your favorite. I like to purchase fresh salsa from the grocery. Also, you can add shrimp or crabmeat to cheesecake for a seafood southwestern version.

1. Preheat oven 350°F. Coat 9-inch spring form pan with nonstick cooking spray.

2. In spring form pan, mix together cereal crumbs, butter, and oil, press into bottom of prepared pan.

3. In mixing bowl, mix together cream cheese, sour cream, egg and egg whites until creamy. Add garlic, chili powder and cumin, mixing well.

4. Fold in Cheddar cheese, green chilies, green onions, and onion. Carefully spread half mixture over crust, top with 1 cup salsa, and cover with remaining cream cheese mixture; do not mix.

5. Bake 50-60 minutes or until mixture is set. Remove from oven, let cool in pan 10 minutes. Run knife around inside edge to loosen, remove sides from pan. Cool to room temperature before refrigerating. When ready to serve, remove from refrigerator and top with remaining 1 cup salsa.

Fiesta Southwestern Cheesecake

A friend is someone who thinks you are a good egg,
even though you are slightly cracked and
sometimes slightly scrambled.

Shrimp Bundles

Great to make ahead and refrigerate until ready to cook. Serve as appetizer, salad topper or as a meal.

Makes 16 shrimp wraps

16 medium-large shrimp, peeled and butterflied

Seasoning salt

2 ounces reduced-fat cream cheese

1/2 teaspoon minced garlic

Salt and pepper to taste

8 slices center cut bacon, cut in half

1/2 cup baby spinach leaves

1. Preheat oven 375°F. Coat baking sheet with nonstick cooking spray.

2. Season shrimp to taste. In small bowl, mix together cream cheese, garlic, salt and pepper; set aside.

3. Lay bacon strips down flat. Place butterfly shrimp on top of bacon. Place spinach leaf or two on shrimp. Divide cream cheese mixture on top of spinach. Wrap bacon around mixture in tight bundle, lay seam side down on baking sheet. If desired, hold with toothpick.

4. Bake 15 - 20 minutes or until shrimp are almost done. Change oven to broil and broil another 2 minutes or until bacon is crispy. Watch carefully.

Nutritional information per serving:

Calories 32

Calories from fat 52%

Fat 2g

Saturated Fat 1g

Cholesterol 27mg

Sodium 108mg

Carbohydrate 0g

Dietary Fiber 0g

Sugars 0g

Protein 4g

Dietary Exchanges: 1/2 lean meat

Spicy Advice

To butterfly shrimp: split shrimp with knife inserted but don't cut all the way, open shrimp to lie flat (two halves).

Spiced Walnuts

These wonderful walnuts with a touch of spice, heat and sweet can be tossed in salads, served on cheese trays or eaten as a snack.

Makes 8 (1/4 cup) servings

2 cups walnut halves

1 tablespoon sugar

1/4 teaspoon salt

1/2 teaspoon garlic powder

1/2 teaspoon ground cumin

1/4 teaspoon ground cinnamon

1/4 teaspoon cayenne pepper

1 tablespoon canola oil

1. Preheat oven 375° F.

2. Spread walnuts on baking sheet and bake about 5-7 minutes or until golden.

3. In small bowl, combine sugar, salt, garlic powder, cumin, cinnamon, and cayenne.

4. In nonstick skillet, heat oil over medium heat. Add nuts and stir to coat with oil. Add seasoning mix, stirring until nuts coated. Remove to paper towel to cool.

Nutritional information per serving:

Calories 99

Calories from fat 46%

Fat 5g

Saturated Fat 1g

Cholesterol 4mg

Sodium 210mg

Carbohydrate 8g

Dietary Fiber 3g

Sugars 4g

Protein 6g

Dietary Exchanges: 1/2 starch, 1 lean meat, 1/2 fat

One Dish Oven Baked French Toast

Medium-Dark Roast

Cross breakfast off your list when you have extras at the house as you can whip up this delicious dish the night before and pop in the oven the next day. It worked when I had 30 college kids at my house for Mardi Gras one year.

Makes 10 servings

1 large loaf French bread
   (whole wheat may be used),
   cut into 1-inch thick squares

1 (10-ounce) jar seedless all natural
   blackberry fruit spread

1 (8-ounce) package reduced-fat
   cream cheese

1/3 cup sugar

1/4 cup skim milk

2 eggs

4 egg whites

1/2 cup light brown sugar

2 cups fat-free half-and-half

1 tablespoon vanilla extract

1 teaspoon ground cinnamon

1. Coat 13×9× 2-inch baking pan with nonstick cooking spray

2. Place half of French bread squares in prepared baking pan. In microwave-safe dish, heat jam until melted, stirring. Drizzle over bread.

3. In bowl, beat together cream cheese, 1/3 cup sugar and milk until smooth. Drop over bread mixture and cover with remaining French bread squares.

4. In large bowl, whisk together eggs, egg whites, brown sugar, half-and-half, vanilla and cinnamon. Pour mixture evenly over bread. Gently press bread into liquid mixture, cover, and refrigerate as time permits, preferably overnight.

5. Preheat oven 325°F. Bake, covered, 30-35 minutes, uncover 5-10 minutes or until bread is golden.

Southwestern Shrimp, Corn, and Sweet Potato Soup

Nutritional information per serving:

Calories 146
Calories from fat 8%
Fat 1g
Saturated Fat 0g
Cholesterol 84mg
Sodium 518mg
Carbohydrate 23g
Dietary Fiber 3g
Sugars 5g
Protein 12g
Dietary Exchanges:
1 1/2 starch, 1 1/2 very lean meat

Naturally sweet yams, shrimp, corn and spicy southwestern seasonings flawlessly come together in this easy (dump and stir) satisfying soup.

Makes 12 (1-cup) servings

1 red onion, chopped

1/2 teaspoon minced garlic

2 cups diced peeled Louisiana yams, (sweet potatoes)

1 (16-ounce) bag frozen corn

1 (15-ounce) can cream-style corn

1 (10-ounce) can chopped tomatoes and green chilies

1 cup salsa

4 cups fat-free chicken broth

2 teaspoons chili powder

1 teaspoon ground cumin

1 1/2 pounds peeled medium shrimp

Salt and pepper to taste

Chopped green onions

1. In large nonstick pot coated with nonstick cooking spray, sauté onion and garlic until tender. Add all ingredients except shrimp; bring mixture to boil.

2. Add shrimp, return to boil, reduce heat and continue cooking until shrimp are done, 7-10 minutes. Season to taste. Sprinkle with green onions, when serving.

Southwestern Shrimp, Corn, and Sweet Potato Soup

Chili Con Carne ❄

**Nutritional information
per serving:**

Calories 285
Calories from fat 20%
Fat 7g
Saturated Fat 2g
Cholesterol 62mg
Sodium 594mg
Carbohydrate 28g
Dietary Fiber 7g
Sugars 12g
Protein 31g
Dietary Exchanges:
1 starch, 3 vegetable, 3 lean meat

Nothing beats chili, especially packed with secret ingredients that explode with flavor, serve with cheese, onions and avocados.

Makes 8 (1-cup) servings

2 pounds ground sirloin or turkey

1 large onion, chopped

1 green bell pepper, cored and chopped

1 tablespoon minced garlic

3 (14 1/2-ounce) cans
   fire-roasted tomatoes

2 tablespoons cocoa

1 teaspoon dried oregano leaves

2 tablespoons chili powder

1 teaspoon ground cumin

1 teaspoon ground cinnamon

1/2 teaspoon ground cloves or allspice

1 tablespoon light brown sugar

1 (15-ounce) can red kidney beans,
   rinsed and drained

1. In large nonstick pot, cook meat, onion, green pepper and garlic over medium heat until meat is done. Drain any excess fat.

2. Add remaining ingredients except beans. Bring to boil, reduce heat, and cook, covered, 30 minutes. Add beans, heat and serve.

Muffaletta Salad

**Nutritional information
per serving:**

Calories 328
Calories from fat 37%
Fat 13g
Saturated Fat 1g
Cholesterol 12mg
Sodium 689mg
Carbohydrate 40g
Dietary Fiber 2g
Sugars 3g
Protein 11g
Dietary Exchanges:
2 starch, 1/2 other carbohydrate,
1 lean meat, 2 fat

All the components of a muffaletta, an Italian signature sandwich of New Orleans, tossed together in an amazing crowd pleasing salad. Olive salad, the key ingredient, is found in a jar- if not available, raid olive salad bar and chop finely.

Makes 8 (1-cup) servings

6 cups cooked orzo pasta

3-4 ounces prosciutto, chopped

1 (14-ounce) can artichoke hearts,
   drained and chopped

1/2 cup chopped roasted red pepper
   (found in jar)

3/4 cup olive salad mix, drained

3/4 cup chopped red onion

1/3 cup crumbled reduced-fat
   feta cheese

1 pound seasoned cooked
   shrimp, optional

1. In large bowl, mix together all ingredients, adding shrimp if desired. Refrigerate until serving.

Cannelloni

I took my friend Alison's famous cannelloni, and cut out tons of calories and fat but left all the flavor! Get organized to easily prepare in a timely manner–boil manicotti, start Tomato Sauce, cook meat and make Cream Sauce-done!

Makes 6- 8 servings

1 (8-ounce) package manicotti shells

1 onion, finely chopped

1 teaspoon minced garlic

1/2 cup finely chopped carrot

1 pound ground sirloin

1 teaspoon dried oregano leaves

1 (10-ounce) package frozen chopped
   spinach, thawed and squeezed dry

1 egg, beaten

2 tablespoons fat-free half-and-half

3 tablespoons grated Parmesan cheese

Salt and pepper to taste

Cream Sauce (recipe follows)

Tomato Sauce (recipe follows)

1. Preheat oven 350ºF. Coat 3-quart baking dish with nonstick cooking spray.

2. Cook manicotti shells according to package directions. Rinse, drain, and set aside.

3. In large nonstick skillet coated with nonstick cooking spray, cook onion, garlic, and carrot over medium heat about 5 minutes. Add meat and continue to cook until done. Add oregano and spinach, mixing well. Cool slightly.

4. In small bowl, whisk together egg and half-and-half. Add egg mixture and cheese to meat, season to taste, mix well. Stuff shells with meat mixture, and arrange in prepared baking dish.

5. Cover with Cream Sauce (see recipe) and top with Tomato Sauce (see recipe). Bake 15 minutes. Uncover, and bake 10 minutes, or until bubbly and well heated.

Cream Sauce

A combination of flour and half-and-half (no butter)
does the trick for a rich creamy white sauce.

1/4 cup all-purpose flour

1/4 cup skim milk

2 cups fat-free half-and-half

Salt and white pepper
to taste

In nonstick pot, whisk together flour, milk and half-and-half.
Heat over medium heat, stirring, until mixture comes to a
boil and thickens. Season to taste.

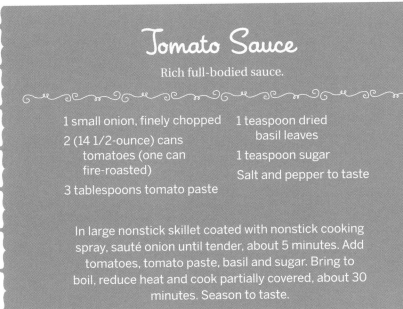

Tomato Sauce

Rich full-bodied sauce.

1 small onion, finely chopped

2 (14 1/2-ounce) cans tomatoes (one can fire-roasted)

3 tablespoons tomato paste

1 teaspoon dried basil leaves

1 teaspoon sugar

Salt and pepper to taste

In large nonstick skillet coated with nonstick cooking spray, sauté onion until tender, about 5 minutes. Add tomatoes, tomato paste, basil and sugar. Bring to boil, reduce heat and cook partially covered, about 30 minutes. Season to taste.

Chicken Enchiladas (pg 128)

Chicken Enchiladas ❄

Nutritional information per serving:

Calories 295
Calories from fat 29%
Fat 9g
Saturated Fat 4g
Cholesterol 49mg
Sodium 995mg
Carbohydrate 31g
Dietary Fiber 3g
Sugars 3g
Protein 20g
Dietary Exchanges:
1 1/2 starch, 1 vegetable,
2 lean meat

Extraordinary homemade enchiladas-one bite and you'll satisfy your Mexican craving without leaving the house. Serve with sliced avocados.

Makes 12 enchiladas

3 cups chopped, cooked chicken breasts

2 cups salsa, divided

1 teaspoon chili powder

6 ounces reduced-fat cream cheese

1 (4-ounce) can green chilies

2/3 cup sliced ripe olives

1 cup chopped green onions

1 3/4 cups canned enchilada sauce, divided

12 (8-inch) flour tortillas (try whole wheat)

1 1/2 cups shredded reduced-fat Mexican blend cheese, divided

Chopped green onions, garnish

Spicy Advice

A great convenience item time-saver is frozen cooked grilled chicken breast-keep in freezer to pull out for ready-to-use chicken with grilled flavor-kicks up chicken flavor in a flash.

1. Preheat oven 350°F. Coat oblong 3-quart baking dish with nonstick cooking spray.

2. In nonstick pot, over medium heat, combine chicken, 1 cup salsa, and chili powder. Add cream cheese, green chilies, and olives, stirring occasionally, until cream cheese melts. Add green onions.

3. Place enchilada sauce in shallow bowl. Lightly dip both sides of tortilla in sauce and spoon about 1/3 cup chicken mixture and 1 tablespoon cheese onto each tortilla. Roll up tightly and place seam-side down in prepared pan. Repeat with remaining tortillas.

4. Combine half remaining enchilada sauce with remaining 1 cup salsa, and spoon over enchiladas. Cover with foil and bake 25-30 minutes or until well heated. Sprinkle with remaining 3/4 cup cheese and return to oven until cheese melts, about 5 minutes. Sprinkle with green onions, if desired.

Southwestern Lasagna

Easy and excellent - go southwestern with lasagna.

Makes 8-10 servings

Nutritional information per serving:

Calories 313
Calories from fat 28%
Fat 10g
Saturated Fat 4g
Cholesterol 53mg
Sodium 846mg
Carbohydrate 28g
Dietary Fiber 1g
Sugars 4g
Protein 29g
Dietary Exchanges:
1 1/2 starch, 1 vegetable,
3 1/2 lean meat

1 1/2 pounds ground sirloin

1 teaspoon minced garlic

1 (16-ounce) jar salsa

1 (19-ounce) can enchilada sauce, divided (about 1 3/4 cup)

Salt and pepper to taste

1 1/2 cups reduced-fat or fat-free cottage cheese

1 egg white

1/2 pound no boil lasagna noodles

1 cup frozen corn, thawed

2 cups shredded reduced-fat Mexican blend cheese

No-boil noodles make lasagna a quick recipe.

1. Preheat oven 350°F. Coat 13x9x2-inch baking dish with nonstick cooking spray

2. In large nonstick skillet, cook meat and garlic over medium heat until done, drain excess fat. Add salsa, and 1 1/4 cups enchilada sauce. Bring to boil, reduce heat, and continue cooking 10 minutes. Season to taste.

3. In food processor, process cottage cheese and egg white until smooth; set aside.

4. Spread thin layer meat sauce in prepared dish. Layer one-third the noodles, all the corn, half the meat sauce, and half the cheese. Repeat with one-third noodles, all cottage cheese mixture, remaining meat, and remaining noodles. Cover with remaining 1/2 cup enchilada sauce and sprinkle with remaining cheese. Bake, covered with foil, 50-60 minutes or until done.

Southwestern Lasagna

Asparagus Wraps

Nutritional information per serving:

Calories 25
Calories from fat 45%
Fat 1g
Saturated Fat 0g
Cholesterol 0mg
Sodium 2mg
Carbohydrate 3g
Dietary Fiber 1g
Sugars 1g
Protein 1g
Dietary Exchanges:
1 vegetable

Spicy Advice

Serve as special side or makes perfect party pick-up.

This unbeatable combination of mellow asparagus with crispy coating, salty prosciutto and a touch of cheese make this a lip-smacking veggie. Can prepare ahead of time, refrigerate and bake before serving- quick with amazing finish.

Makes 10-12 servings

24 asparagus spears (about 1 pound), trimmed discarding ends

8 sheets of phyllo dough, thawed

1/4 cup grated Parmesan cheese

3 ounces prosciutto, cut into strips

1. Preheat oven 425°F. Coat foil lined baking sheet with nonstick cooking spray.

2. Cook asparagus in large skillet with little water until tender, about 3-5 minutes depending on size of asparagus (or can cook in microwave).

3. Take two sheets phyllo dough and coat each sheet with nonstick cooking spray and layer. Cut into 6 sections (one across and two down).

4. Sprinkle each section with about 1/2 teaspoon Parmesan. Wrap prosciutto strip around asparagus. Lay asparagus on corner of phyllo section and roll up, diagonally, exposing asparagus tip. Transfer to prepared pan. Repeat with remaining asparagus. Coat asparagus with nonstick cooking spray.

5. Bake 8-10 minutes or until phyllo is golden and crispy. Serve warm or room temperature. For thin asparagus, use two instead of one for each wrap.

Asparagus Wraps

Asparagus with Zucchini Rings

Nutritional information per serving:

Calories 50
Calories from fat 45%
Fat 3g
Saturated Fat 0g
Cholesterol 0mg
Sodium 4mg
Carbohydrate 5g
Dietary Fiber 2g
Sugars 3g
Protein 2g
Dietary Exchanges:
1 vegetable, 1/2 fat

This veggie captivated my attention at a dinner for 300 people so I went home to make them. Simple ingredients, eye-catching and unbelievably delicious- they add flair and flavor to any plate. Make ahead, refrigerate, and cook when ready to serve.

Makes 10 bundles

1 medium zucchini

1 pound asparagus, trimmed discarding ends

1-2 tablespoons olive oil

Salt and pepper to taste

1. Preheat oven 400°F. Coat foil lined baking sheet with nonstick cooking spray.

2. Cut zucchini into 1/4-inch diagonal slices and hollow out hole in center of each slice, leaving an edge (like napkin ring). Place about 3 asparagus, depending on size through hole, and lay on baking sheet.

3. Drizzle with olive oil and season to taste. Roast 25-30 minutes or until tender and browned.

Asparagus with Zucchini Rings

Sweet Potato Wedges Wrapped in Prosciutto

Nutritional information per serving:

Calories 152
Calories from fat 12%
Fat 2g
Saturated Fat 1g
Cholesterol 12mg
Sodium 313mg
Carbohydrate 29g
Dietary Fiber 3g
Sugars 11g
Protein 5g
Dietary Exchanges:
2 starch

I prepared these show-stopper potatoes for company one evening. Prepare ahead of time, refrigerate, and bake when ready to serve. Impressive and savor that sweet-salty combination.

Makes 8 wedges

2 Louisiana yams (sweet potatoes), (about 2 pounds)

Fresh basil leaves

4 ounces prosciutto, trimmed and slice in half lengthwise

1/4 cup pure maple syrup

1. Preheat oven 425°F. Coat oblong baking dish with nonstick cooking spray.

2. Peel and cut sweet potatoes into wedges (four per potato). In large nonstick skillet, add water to cover sweet potatoes. Bring to boil, cook 8-10 minutes or only until potatoes are firm but cooked. Do not overcook as will fall apart. Drain.

3. Lay basil leaf on potato wedge and wrap with prosciutto. Repeat with all sweet potato wedges. Lay in prepared baking dish.

4. Drizzle with maple syrup, bake 10 minutes or until prosciutto starts to crisp.

At a dinner party one should eat wisely but not too well, **and talk well but not too wisely.**

Eggnog Spice Bundt Cake

Espresso

This marvelous moist cake melts in your mouth. Spice and everything nice makes this a holiday hit.

Makes 16-20 servings

Nutritional information per serving:

Calories 256
Calories from fat 39%
Fat 12g
Saturated Fat 4g
Cholesterol 16mg
Sodium 268mg
Carbohydrate 36g
Dietary Fiber 0g
Sugars 25g
Protein 4g
Dietary Exchanges:
2 1/2 other carbohydrate,
2 fat

1 (18.25-ounce) box spice cake mix
1 (4-serving) box instant cheesecake pudding and pie filling mix
1 cup vanilla or eggnog nonfat yogurt
1/4 cup canola oil
1 cup light eggnog

1 egg
3 egg whites
1 cup butterscotch chips
2/3 cup chopped pecans

1. Preheat oven 350°F. Coat nonstick Bundt pan with nonstick cooking spray.

2. In mixing bowl, combine cake mix, pudding mix, yogurt, oil, eggnog, egg, and egg whites, mixing until creamy.

3. Stir in butterscotch chips and pecans. Pour in prepared pan and bake 40-45 minutes or until toothpick inserted comes out clean.

Outrageous Ice Cream Dessert

Medium-Dark Roast

The name says it all—and the best part is it's freezer friendly and knock-out simple!

Makes 12 servings

Nutritional information per serving:

Calories 237
Calories from fat 6%
Fat 2g
Saturated Fat 1g
Cholesterol 3mg
Sodium 163mg
Carbohydrate 51g
Dietary Fiber 4g
Sugars 27g
Protein 2g
Dietary Exchanges:
3 1/2 other carbohydrate,
1/2 fat

12 low fat vanilla ice cream sandwiches
1 (8-ounce) container fat-free frozen whipped topping, thawed, divided
2 large bananas, divided

6 tablespoons caramel/butterscotch topping, divided
4 tablespoons chocolate topping, divided

1. In a 9x9x2-inch glass dish, place 6 ice cream sandwiches along the bottom.

2. Layer with half the whipped topping, one sliced banana, and drizzle with half each of the toppings. Repeat layers and freeze overnight (if you have time).

Holiday Bars

Medium-Dark Roast

Holiday ingredients create an easy festive bar cookie.

48 servings

Nutritional information per serving:

Calories 57
Calories from fat 42%
Fat 3g
Saturated Fat 1g
Cholesterol 4mg
Sodium 34mg
Carbohydrate 8g
Dietary Fiber 0g
Sugars 6g
Protein 1g
Dietary Exchanges:
1/2 other carbohydrate, 1/2 fat

1 1/2 cups gingersnap crumbs
6 tablespoons butter, melted
1 teaspoon vanilla extract
1/2 cup dried cranberries

1/3 cup white chocolate chips
1/3 cup chopped pecans
2/3 cup of (14-ounce) can fat-free sweetened condensed milk

1. Preheat oven 350° F. Coat 13x9x2-inch pan with nonstick cooking spray.

2. In prepared pan, mix gingersnaps, butter, and vanilla; press into pan.

3. Sprinkle cranberries, white chocolate chips, and pecans evenly over gingersnap crust. Drizzle sweetened condensed milk over top. Bake 15-20 minutes or until bubbly and light brown.

Isn't it coincidental wine improves with age,
age improves with wine?

Coffee Punch

Flavored Coffee

Coffee drinkers or not, adore this trendy tasting frosty ice cream-coffee punch. Serve in punch bowl or in pitcher with bowls of whipped topping and cocoa.

Makes 24-30 servings

2 quarts brewed coffee (flavored or decaffeinated coffee may be used), cooled to room temperature

3/4 cup sugar

1 tablespoon vanilla extract

2 cups fat-free half-and-half

2 quarts fat-free vanilla ice cream or frozen vanilla yogurt, softened

1 (8-ounce) container frozen fat-free whipped topping, thawed

Cocoa, optional for sprinkling

1. In large container, combine cooled coffee, sugar and vanilla. Refrigerate until well chilled or overnight.

2. When ready to serve, combine coffee mixture and half-and-half. In punch bowl, place ice cream and pour coffee milk mixture on top.

3. Serve with dollop of whipped topping and sprinkle with cocoa.

Nutritional information per serving:
Calories 98
Calories from fat 0%
Fat 0g
Saturated Fat 0g
Cholesterol 0mg
Sodium 56mg
Carbohydrate 22g
Dietary Fiber 0g
Sugars 15g
Protein 3g
Dietary Exchanges:
1 1/2 other carbohydrate

COFFEE CONDIMENT SERVING DISH

Everyone in the south has a deviled egg dish - so fill with your favorite fun coffee condiments to serve with coffee.

Summer Limeade

Nutritional information
per serving:

Calories 190
Calories from fat 0%
Fat 0g
Saturated Fat 0g
Cholesterol 0mg
Sodium 2mg
Carbohydrate 49g
Dietary Fiber 1g
Sugars 44g
Protein 1g
Dietary Exchanges:
3 other carbohydrate

Have leftover watermelon-create a refreshing fruity frappe-style summer drink. For an alcoholic version, add some rum or vodka.

Makes 7 (1-cup) servings

3 1/2-4 cups small chunks watermelon or 3 cups pureed watermelon

1 pint strawberries, hulled

1/4 cup sugar

1 (12-ounce) can frozen limeade, thawed

3/4 cup lemon juice

1 cup water

Mint to garnish, optional

1. In food processor, puree watermelon in batches until smooth; remove and pour into 2-quart pitcher.

2. In food processor, process strawberries with sugar until smooth. Transfer to pitcher, and add limeade, lemon juice, and water, mixing well. Refrigerate and serve over ice with sprig of mint.

Pomegranate Champagne Punch

Nutritional information
per serving:

Calories 235
Calories from fat 0%
Fat 0g
Saturated Fat 0g
Cholesterol 0mg
Sodium 11mg
Carbohydrate 46g
Dietary Fiber 0g
Sugars 43g
Protein 0g
Dietary Exchanges:
3 other carbohydrate

Move over Mimosas as this is the perfect punch for any celebration or time of day.

Makes 8 (1-cup) servings

1 bottle Champagne

1 cup pomegranate juice

1 1/2 cups sugar

3 cups water

1 cup lemon juice

1. In large pot, combine all ingredients and bring to a boil. Cool and refrigerate until serving.

Pomegranate Margarita Martini

Nutritional information per serving:

Calories 118
Calories from fat 0%
Fat 0g
Saturated Fat 0g
Cholesterol 0mg
Sodium 3mg
Carbohydrate 24g
Dietary Fiber 0g
Sugars 17g
Protein 0g
Dietary Exchanges:
1 1/2 other carbohydrate

Pomegranate and margaritas pair up with a martini for a dose of fun and antioxidants. No bartenders needed as I served this easy- to- make drink in a pitcher. Be sure to make a big batch as I had to go back and make more.

Makes 3 cups

2 cups alcoholic margarita mix

1/2 cup pomegranate juice

1/4 cup tequila

1/4 cup lime juice

1 In a pitcher, mix together all ingredients. Serve over ice or in martini glass.

Cranberry Margarita Tea

Nutritional information per serving:

Calories 173
Calories from fat 0%
Fat 0g
Saturated Fat 0g
Cholesterol 0mg
Sodium 2mg
Carbohydrate 45g
Dietary Fiber 0g
Sugars 40g
Protein 3g
Dietary Exchanges:
3 other carbohydrate

Tea has never made you feel this good! A light refreshing drink. Any tea may be used.

Makes 6 (1-cup) servings

1 (20-ounce) bottle green tea with honey

2 1/2 cups cranberry juice cocktail

1 cup alcoholic margarita mix

1/4 cup honey

Fresh cranberries for garnish

1 In a pitcher, mix together all ingredients. Mix well and refrigerate. Serve over ice.

Brunch & Munch

Fruits and vegetables are important to include in your morning meal. I suggest **carrot bread, zucchini bread, strawberry bread, banana bread,** and **sweet potato pancakes.**

Mexican Breakfast Casserole

Medium-Light
Roast

Simple ingredients magically create this make-ahead scrumptious breakfast dish fulfilling everyone's expectations in my house.

Makes 8-10 servings

1 (4-ounce) can green chilies

8 ounces ground breakfast
   turkey sausage

1 onion, chopped

1 red, green, or yellow bell
   pepper, cored and chopped

1 teaspoon minced garlic

1 tablespoon chili powder

5 eggs

4 egg whites

2 cups fat-free half-and-half

1/2 cup chopped green onions

1 1/2 cups reduced-fat shredded
   Mexican blend cheese

5 (8-inch) 98% fat-free flour tortillas,
   cut into quarters

1. Coat 13x9x2-inch baking dish with nonstick cooking spray. Spread green chilies along bottom of dish.

2. In large nonstick skillet, cook and crumble sausage until starts to brown. Add onion and bell pepper, cooking until sausage is done and vegetables tender. Add garlic and chili powder. Remove from heat. Cool.

3. In large bowl, whisk together eggs, egg whites, and half-and-half. In another bowl, combine green onion and cheese.

4. Spoon one-third of sausage mixture over chilies in baking dish. Top with one-third tortilla quarters and one-third cheese mixture. Repeat layers, ending with cheese. Pour egg mixture evenly over casserole and refrigerate, covered, at least 6 hours or overnight.

5. Preheat oven 350°F. If using glass baking dish, place in cold oven and bake 50-60 minutes or until bubbly and golden brown and knife inserted into custard comes out clean.

Mexican Breakfast Casserole

Breakfast Pizza

Medium Roast

Looking for an easy and excellent way to start the morning? With crescent roll crust, sausage, hash browns, cheese and egg filling, this recipe rocks! Fun, filling and fantastic!

Makes 8 servings

1 (8-ounce) can reduced-fat
    crescent rolls

12 ounces ground breakfast
    turkey sausage

1 cup frozen shredded hash brown
    potatoes, thawed

1 cup shredded reduced-fat
    Cheddar cheese

1/4 cup skim milk

3 eggs

3 egg whites

Salt and pepper to taste

1/4 cup chopped green onions

1. Preheat oven 375°F. Coat 12-inch pizza pan with nonstick cooking spray.

2. Separate crescent rolls into triangles. Press triangles together (points toward the center) to form crust on pizza pan. Bottom crust should be sealed and crimp outside edges of dough to form a rim. Crust will not cover to end of pan.

3. In large nonstick skillet, cook sausage until done, and crumble. Drain. Top prepared dough with sausage, potatoes, and cheese.

4. In bowl, whisk together milk, eggs, egg whites and season to taste. Carefully and slowly pour egg mixture evenly over sausage mixture. Sprinkle with green onions. Bake 25 minutes or until crust is browned.

**Nutritional information
per serving:**

Calories 242
Calories from fat 39%
Fat 10g
Saturated Fat 5g
Cholesterol 108mg
Sodium 615mg
Carbohydrate 18g
Dietary Fiber 0g
Sugars 3g
Protein 17g
Dietary Exchanges:
1 starch, 2 lean meat, 1/2 fat

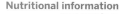

Spicy Advice

Serve with fresh fruit.

Sweet Potato Praline Pancakes

Medium-Light Roast

Make a batch of these fantastic pancakes, freeze and pop in microwave for quick breakfast. Serve with maple syrup and top with toasted pecans, if desired.

Makes 16 pancakes

1 cup mashed sweet potatoes (Louisiana yams) or 1 (15-ounce) can sweet potatoes, drained and mashed

1 2/3 cups skim milk

2 eggs

1 tablespoon canola oil

1 teaspoon vanilla extract

1 cup all-purpose or whole wheat flour (or combination)

1/2 cup old fashioned oatmeal

3 tablespoons light brown sugar

1 tablespoon baking powder

1 teaspoon baking soda

1 teaspoon ground cinnamon

1/8 teaspoon ground nutmeg

1/4 cup pecans, toasted

1. In large bowl, mix together sweet potatoes, milk, eggs, oil and vanilla.

2. In small bowl, combine flour, oatmeal, brown sugar, baking powder, baking soda, cinnamon and nutmeg. Add dry ingredients and pecans to sweet potato mixture, stirring just until combined.

3. Heat large nonstick skillet coated with nonstick cooking spray over medium heat. Using 1/4 cup batter per pancake, cook pancakes 1-2 minutes on each side or until lightly browned. Recoat pan between pancakes.

The whole wheat flour and oatmeal boost the fiber and add a nutty flavor.

Sweet Potato Praline Pancakes

Carrot Pineapple Bread

Wow, this winning combination with pineapple, carrots, coconut and walnuts packs flavors and textures.

Makes 16 servings

1/3 cup canola oil

3/4 cup sugar

2 eggs

1 cup all-purpose flour

1/2 cup whole wheat flour or
   all-purpose flour

1 1/4 teaspoons baking powder

1/2 teaspoon baking soda

1 teaspoon ground cinnamon

1 (8-ounce) can crushed pineapple
   in juice, drained

1 cup grated carrots

1/3 cup flaked coconut

1/3 cup chopped walnuts, toasted

1. Preheat oven 350°F. Coat 9x5x3-inch nonstick loaf pan with nonstick cooking spray.

2. In mixing bowl, mix together oil and sugar. Gradually add eggs, beating well.

3. In bowl, combine both flours, baking powder, baking soda, and cinnamon and add alternately with crushed pineapple to sugar mixture, stirring only until combined. Stir in carrots, coconut and walnuts. Transfer batter to prepared pan.

4. Bake 35-40 minutes or until toothpick comes out clean.

Spicy Advice

Coconut may be left out of any bread if you're not a coconut fan — I want coconut in everything.

I'm really in the mood for a QUICKIE. It's pronounced "Quiche." *In that case, I'll have a salad.*

Perky Chocolate Zucchini Bread

No energy? Perk up your morning with chocolate and coffee for an extra jolt. I add chocolate chips — more chocolate, the better — after all, it's for energy.

Makes 16 slices

1 1/2 cups all-purpose flour

1/4 cup cocoa

1 teaspoon baking soda

1/2 teaspoon baking powder

1 teaspoon ground cinnamon

1 cup light brown sugar

2 eggs

1/3 cup canola oil

1 teaspoon vanilla extract

1 teaspoon instant dark roast or espresso coffee dissolved in 1 teaspoon warm water

1/4 cup skim milk

1 1/2 cups shredded zucchini

1/2 cup chopped pecans or walnuts

1/3 cup semi-sweet chocolate chips, optional

Brewed strong coffee may be substituted for milk, if you don't have instant dark roast.

1. Preheat oven 350°F. Coat 9x5x3-inch nonstick loaf pan with nonstick cooking spray.

2. In bowl, combine flour, cocoa, baking soda, baking powder, and cinnamon: set aside.

3. In medium bowl, mix brown sugar, eggs, oil, vanilla and coffee until well blended.

4. Add dry ingredients alternately with the milk and stir until just moistened. Stir in remaining ingredients. Transfer batter into prepared pan.

5. Bake 40-50 minutes. Don't overbake as cooks more when cooling.

Perky Chocolate Zucchini Bread

Banana Chocolate Chip Bread

Medium Roast

Nutritional information per serving:

Calories 221
Calories from fat 33%
Fat 8g
Saturated Fat 2g
Cholesterol 26mg
Sodium 131mg
Carbohydrate 35g
Dietary Fiber 2g
Sugars 19g
Protein 4g
Dietary Exchanges:
2 1/2 other carbohydrate, 1 1/2 fat

Turn ripe bananas into this unbeatable bread that boasts bananas, crunchy nuts, coconut and rich dark chocolate in every bite.

Makes 16 slices

1/2 cup sugar	2 cups all-purpose flour
1/4 cup honey	1 1/2 teaspoon baking soda
1/4 cup canola oil	1/3 cup chopped walnuts
2 eggs	1/4 cup flaked coconut
4 ripe bananas, mashed	1/2 cup dark chocolate chips
1 teaspoon vanilla extract	

1. Preheat oven 350°F. Coat 9x5x3-inch nonstick loaf pan with nonstick cooking spray.

2. In large bowl, mix together sugar, honey, oil, eggs, mashed banana and vanilla.

3. In another bowl, combine flour and baking soda. Add flour mixture to banana mixture, mixing only until combined. Stir in walnuts, coconut and chocolate chips. Transfer batter to prepared pan.

4. Bake about 50 minutes or until toothpick inserted in center comes out clean. Don't overcook.

In any bread recipe, use a combination of whole-wheat flour and all-purpose to boost the nutritional value. Did you know you can freeze ripe bananas to later use in banana bread?

If you want breakfast in bed,
sleep in the kitchen.

Strawberry Bread

Nutritional information per serving:

Calories 141
Calories from fat 28%
Fat 4g
Saturated Fat 3g
Cholesterol 24mg
Sodium 113mg
Carbohydrate 23g
Dietary Fiber 1g
Sugars 11g
Protein 2g
Dietary Exchanges:
1 1/2 other carbohydrate,
1 fat

Strawberries with a touch of lemon combine together for the best berry bread. Any red fruit juice may be used for cranberry-strawberry juice.

Makes 16 servings

2 cups all-purpose flour

3/4 cup sugar

1 1/2 teaspoons baking powder

1/2 teaspoon baking soda

1 egg

1 egg white

1/3 cup butter, melted

1/3 cup cranberry-strawberry juice

2 teaspoons grated lemon rind

1 1/2 cups strawberries, hulled and coarsely chopped

1. Preheat oven 350° F. Coat 9x5x3-inch nonstick loaf pan with nonstick cooking spray.

2. In large bowl, mix together flour, sugar, baking powder, and baking soda. In small bowl, whisk egg and egg white. Stir in melted butter, juice, and lemon rind.

3. Add to flour mixture, stirring until well combined. Stir in strawberries. Transfer batter to prepared pan.

4. Bake 50-60 minutes, or until toothpick inserted in center comes out clean; cover loosely with foil if it browns too fast.

Strawberry Bread

Quick Lemon Blueberry Bread

Nutritional information per serving:

Calories 164
Calories from fat 24%
Fat 4g
Saturated Fat 2g
Cholesterol 37mg
Sodium 200mg
Carbohydrate 28g
Dietary Fiber 1g
Sugars 20g
Protein 3g
Dietary Exchanges:
2 other carbohydrate, 1 fat

Spicy Advice

If using frozen blueberries, do not thaw before using, or the blueberries turn too mushy.

Blueberries burst with flavor and nutrition! This luscious lemon bread is my "go to" easy favorite; in fact, close your eyes and you'll think you are eating cake.

Makes 16 servings

1 (8-ounce) package reduced-fat cream cheese

1 1/3 cups sugar, divided

2 eggs

1 tablespoon lemon extract

1 1/2 cups reduced-fat or regular biscuit baking mix

1 tablespoon grated lemon rind

1 1/2 cups blueberries

1/3 cup lemon juice

1. Preheat oven 350°F. Coat 9x5x3-inch nonstick loaf pan with nonstick cooking spray.

2. In large mixing bowl, mix together cream cheese and 1 cup sugar until light and fluffy. Beat in eggs and lemon extract.

3. Stir in baking mix and lemon rind just until blended. Carefully stir in blueberries. Transfer batter to prepared pan. Bake 50-60 minutes or until toothpick inserted comes out clean.

4. Immediately poke holes in 1-inch intervals on top of bread with toothpick. In microwave-safe dish, combine remaining 1/3 cup sugar and lemon juice, heating until sugar is dissolved. Pour evenly over top of bread. Cool and slice.

Quick Lemon Blueberry Bread

Pull Apart Cinnamon Bread

Flavored Coffee

Nutritional information per serving:

Calories 262
Calories from fat 33%
Fat 10g
Saturated Fat 3g
Cholesterol 8mg
Sodium 541mg
Carbohydrate 41g
Dietary Fiber 1g
Sugars 17g
Protein 4g
Dietary Exchanges:
2 1/2 other carbohydrate,
2 fat

How easy it is to snip biscuits, shake in cinnamon and sugar and the result is this exquisite pull apart bread laced with pecans and cranberries. Great for last minute company, a holiday get together, or to satisfy your morning sweet tooth.

Makes 16 servings

6 tablespoons sugar

2 teaspoons ground cinnamon

3 (12-ounce) cans refrigerated biscuits

1/2 cup chopped pecans

1/3 cup dried cranberries

1/4 cup butter

1/2 cup light brown sugar

1. Preheat oven 350°F. Coat nonstick Bundt pan with nonstick cooking spray.

2. In resealable plastic bag, mix sugar and cinnamon. Cut one can biscuits into quarters and shake with cinnamon mixture in bag. Arrange coated biscuit quarters in bottom of prepared pan.

3. Sprinkle with half pecans and cranberries. Cut another can biscuits into quarters, shake in sugar-cinnamon mixture, arrange on top biscuits. Sprinkle with remaining cranberries and pecans, top with last can quartered biscuits with sugar-cinnamon mixture.

4. In microwave-safe container, microwave butter and brown sugar one minute. Remove, stir and return to microwave another minute or until boiling. Pour evenly over biscuits.

5. Bake 35 minutes. Let sit in pan 5 minutes then invert onto serving plate.

Yummy Yam Praline Coffee Cake

Medium-Dark Roast

This melt-in-your mouth coffeecake starts with a time-honored family pantry staple, biscuit baking mix. My personal favorite recipe — love the naturally sweet yams with the tart cranberries.

Makes 16 servings

2 tablespoons butter, melted

1/2 cup plus 3 tablespoons light brown sugar, divided

2 tablespoons light corn syrup

1/2 cup chopped pecans

2 1/2 cups biscuit baking mix

1 (15-ounce) can sweet potatoes, drained and mashed or 1 cup mashed Louisiana yams (sweet potatoes)

1/3 cup skim milk

1 teaspoon ground cinnamon

1/4 cup dried cranberries

① Preheat oven 400°F. Coat 9x9x2-square baking pan with nonstick baking spray.

② In bottom of prepared pan, mix together butter, 1/2 cup brown sugar and corn syrup. Spread mixture evenly in pan. Sprinkle with pecans.

③ In large mixing bowl, beat together biscuit baking mix, sweet potatoes, and milk until dough forms a ball. Turn dough onto surface heavily dusted with baking mix and roll or pat into 12-inch long rectangle.

④ In small bowl, combine remaining 3 tablespoons brown sugar and cinnamon. Sprinkle brown sugar mixture and cranberries evenly over dough. Roll up dough jellyroll style from longer side. Cut crosswise into one-inch pieces and arrange sitting on top of the pecan mixture in pan. Dough will spread when baking.

⑤ Bake 25-30 minutes or until golden brown. Remove from oven and immediately run knife around sides and invert onto serving plate, scraping any brown sugar mixture from pan to top cake.

Spicy Advice

Don't let this dough intimidate you as it's so easy to work with- can pat out with hands!

Tessa's Cheesecake Squares

Flavored Coffee

Nutritional information per serving:

Calories 99
Calories from fat 44%
Fat 5g
Saturated Fat 3g
Cholesterol 7mg
Sodium 189mg
Carbohydrate 12g
Dietary Fiber 0g
Sugars 5g
Protein 2g
Dietary Exchanges:
1 other carbohydrate,
1 fat

Between a cheesecake and brunch pick up, these easy melt-in-your-mouth squares are so simple to make. Great warm out of the oven, refrigerated, or room temperature.

Makes 24 servings

2 (8-ounce) cans reduced-fat crescent rolls

1 (8-ounce) package reduced-fat cream cheese

1/3 cup sugar plus 1 tablespoon sugar, divided

1 teaspoon vanilla extract

1 teaspoon almond extract

1 teaspoon ground cinnamon

1. Preheat oven 350°F. Coat 13x9x2-inch baking pan with nonstick cooking spray.

2. Press one can crescent rolls into bottom of pan, sealing perforations to form crust.

3. In bowl, mix together cream cheese, 1/3 cup sugar, vanilla and almond extracts until smooth and creamy. Carefully spread over crescent layer.

4. Unroll other can crescent rolls and lay on top cream cheese layer. Don't press down. Mix together remaining 1 tablespoon sugar and cinnamon; sprinkle on top.

5. Bake 25-30 minutes or until top is golden and crisp. Let sit 10 minutes before cutting. Refrigerate, if not serving immediately.

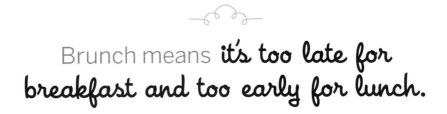

Brunch means *it's too late for breakfast and too early for lunch.*

Morning Muffins

Start your morning off nutritiously and deliciously with all my favorites!

Makes 24 muffins

Nutritional information per serving:

Calories 125
Calories from fat 33%
Fat 5g
Saturated Fat 1g
Cholesterol 18mg
Sodium 138mg
Carbohydrate 19g
Dietary Fiber 1g
Sugars 7g
Protein 3g
Dietary Exchanges:
1 1/2 starch, 1 fat

1 1/2 cups all-purpose flour
1/2 cup whole-wheat flour
3/4 cup old-fashioned oatmeal
1/2 cup light brown sugar
2 teaspoons baking soda
1 teaspoon baking powder
2 teaspoons ground cinnamon
1 teaspoon ground ginger
1 1/2 cups shredded carrots

1/3 cup golden raisins
1/2 cup mashed bananas
2 eggs
1 cup skim milk
1 tablespoon lemon juice
1/4 cup canola oil
1 teaspoon vanilla extract
1/2 cup chopped walnuts

1. Preheat oven 350°F.

2. In large bowl, mix flours, oatmeal, brown sugar, baking soda, baking powder, cinnamon and ginger. Stir in carrots, raisins and banana.

3. In separate bowl, whisk together eggs, milk, lemon juice, oil and vanilla. Add liquids to dry ingredients, stir until moistened. Stir in walnuts. Pour batter into paper lined tins, filling 1/2-3/4 full. Bake 20 minutes, or until golden brown.

Morning Muffins

Blueberry Muffin Streusel Cake

Medium-Dark Roast

My friend, Teresa, gave me this recipe that has been in her family for years. A cross between a muffin and cake; here's my version that I made, again, again, and again — that's how good it is.

Makes 12 servings

1 cup all-purpose flour
1 1/2 teaspoons baking powder
1/2 cup sugar
1/2 cup skim milk

1 egg
2 tablespoons canola oil
1 cup fresh blueberries
Streusel Topping (recipe follows)

1. Preheat oven 375°F. Coat 9x9x2-inch square pan with nonstick cooking spray
2. In bowl, mix together flour, baking powder, sugar, milk and egg.
3. Stir in oil and blueberries, only until mixed.
4. Sprinkle 1/2 cup reserved Streusel Topping (see recipe) on bottom of pan. Carefully spread cake mixture on top. Cover with remaining reserved Streusel Pecan Topping.
5. Bake 20-25 minutes or until toothpick inserted in middle comes out dry.

Spicy Advice

Don't like pecans- leave them out but remember they are a good dose of antioxidants.

Streusel Topping
A perfect topping to any breakfast cake.

1/3 cup sugar
1/3 cup light brown sugar
1/2 cup all-purpose flour
2 teaspoons ground cinnamon

1 teaspoon vanilla extract
3 tablespoons butter, softened
1/2 cup chopped pecans

In small bowl, mix together sugar, brown sugar, flour and cinnamon. Cut in vanilla and butter using pastry blender or fork. Reserve 1/2 cup topping and add pecans to remaining topping.

Sweet Potato Cornmeal Biscuits

Nutritional information per serving:

Calories 121
Calories from fat 18%
Fat 2g
Saturated Fat 1g
Cholesterol 6mg
Sodium 96mg
Carbohydrate 22g
Dietary Fiber 1g
Sugars 4g
Protein 3g
Dietary Exchanges:
1 1/2 starch

An unbeatable biscuit with crispy outside and moist slightly sweet center is made with a non-intimidating- simply pat into a square, cut and bake dough.

Makes 16 biscuits

2 cups all-purpose flour

1/3 cup yellow cornmeal

2 1/2 teaspoons baking powder

3 tablespoons butter, cut into small pieces

1 (15-ounce) can sweet potatoes (Louisiana yams) drained and mashed or 1 cup mashed cooked sweet potato

1/2 cup skim milk

2 tablespoons honey

1. Preheat oven 400°F. Coat baking sheet with nonstick cooking spray.

2. In large bowl, combine flour, cornmeal and baking powder. Cut in butter with pastry blender or fork until mixture looks like coarse meal. Add sweet potato, milk, and honey, stir until just combined.

3. Turn dough onto heavily floured work surface, knead lightly only 5 times. Pat dough into 9-inch square, cut into 16 squares.

4. Place biscuits on prepared pan. Bake 15-20 minutes or until golden brown.

Easy Biscuits

Flavored Coffee

Nutritional information per serving:

Calories 80
Calories from fat 15%
Fat 1g
Saturated Fat 0g
Cholesterol 0mg
Sodium 238mg
Carbohydrate 15g
Dietary Fiber 0g
Sugars 2g
Protein 2g
Dietary Exchanges:
1 starch

Have a craving for homemade biscuits? Try this three ingredient recipe and enjoy the wonderful alluring aroma of home-style baked biscuits.

Makes 18 biscuits

3 cups all purpose reduced-fat or regular biscuit baking mix

1/2 cup nonfat plain yogurt

1/2 cup diet lemon-lime cold drink

1. Preheat oven 450°F. Coat baking sheet with nonstick cooking spray.

2. In large bowl, combine biscuit baking mix, yogurt and lemon-lime cold drink until thoroughly mixed.

3. Knead a few minutes, roll out on floured surface 1/2-inch thick. Cut with 2-inch glass or cookie cutter, place on prepared pan. Bake 8-10 minutes.

Caramel Popcorn Peanut Bars

Nutritional information per serving:

Calories 74
Calories from fat 47%
Fat 4g
Saturated Fat 1g
Cholesterol 3mg
Sodium 8mg
Carbohydrate 9g
Dietary Fiber 1g
Sugars 5g
Protein 1g
Dietary Exchanges:
1/2 other carbohydrate,
1 fat

Popcorn, peanuts, and oatmeal with caramel syrup make a snack that tosses my willpower out the door. Great for kids and adults, easy to make.

Makes 42-48 squares

1 1/2 cups old fashioned oatmeal

1 cup dry roasted peanuts

4 tablespoons butter

2 tablespoons canola oil

2/3 cup light brown sugar

1/3 cup honey

1/2 teaspoon vanilla extract

12 cups popped popcorn

1. Preheat oven 350° F.

2. Place oatmeal and peanuts on baking sheet and bake 12-14 minutes.

3. In medium pot, combine butter, oil, brown sugar and honey over medium heat, stirring until mixture comes to boil. Boil 1 1/2 minutes. Remove from heat and add vanilla.

4. Place popcorn in large bowl and pour hot syrup mixture over popcorn, stirring until coated. Add oatmeal and peanuts, mixing well. Transfer mixture to 15x10x1-inch baking pan lined with foil and coated with nonstick cooking spray and press into pan. Cool, cut into squares. Store in airtight container.

Caramel Popcorn Peanut Bars

Fill Up with Fiber

The difference between a fruit and a vegetable? If you let fruit rot, it turns into wine, something Brussels sprouts never do.

Eggplant Dip

Eggplant and a medley of unusual flavors define this dynamic dip-and wait until you get all the recipe requests! Serve with pita chips.

Makes 8 (1/4-cup) servings

Nutritional information per serving:

Calories 56
Calories from fat 12%
Fat 1g
Saturated Fat 0g
Cholesterol 0mg
Sodium 190mg
Carbohydrate 12g
Dietary Fiber 4g
Sugars 7g
Protein 1g
Dietary Exchanges:
2 vegetable

1 (1 1/2-pound) eggplant

1-2 tablespoons minced fresh ginger or 1 teaspoon ground ginger

1 teaspoon minced garlic

1 teaspoon sweet chili garlic sauce

2 tablespoons light brown sugar

2 tablespoons low sodium soy sauce

2 tablespoons seasoned rice vinegar

1 bunch green onions, chopped

1 cup chopped Roma tomatoes

1 teaspoons sesame oil

Salt and pepper to taste

1. Preheat oven 425°F. Cover baking sheet with foil.

2. Pierce eggplant all over with fork and lay on foil. Roast until eggplant is very soft and deflated, turning once, about 1 hour. Cool slightly.

3. Cut eggplant in half and scrape flesh into strainer to drain about 30 minutes. Transfer eggplant to food processor and process until almost smooth. Transfer to bowl.

4. To eggplant, add ginger and garlic. In microwave-safe container, heat chili garlic sauce, brown sugar and soy sauce about 1 minute or just until boiling; stirring to melt brown sugar. Add to eggplant and stir in remaining ingredients. Serve immediately or refrigerate, covered, until ready to serve. Serve at room temperature.

Spicy Advice

May be prepared 1 day ahead of time.

Best Barley Soup

Terrific twist to basic barley soup with bacon, naturally sweet yams, earthy mushrooms and carrots creating a comforting and soup-erb soup.

Makes 11 (1-cup) servings

5 slices turkey bacon

1/2 pound sliced mushrooms

1 teaspoon minced garlic

1 red onion, chopped

1/2 teaspoon dried thyme leaves

8 cups fat-free chicken broth

1 bay leaf

2 cups chopped carrots

2 cups chopped Louisiana yams (sweet potatoes), peeled and cut into small cubes

3/4 cup medium pearl barley

1. In large nonstick pot, cook bacon until crisp. Remove to paper towels, crumble, set aside.

2. In same pot coated with nonstick cooking spray, sauté mushrooms, garlic, and onion until tender about 7 minutes.

3. Add thyme, broth, bay leaf, carrots, sweet potatoes and barley. Bring to boil, reduce heat, cover, and cook 25 minutes or until barley and vegetables are tender. Season to taste, remove bay leaf. If too thick, add more broth. To serve, sprinkle with crumbled bacon.

Best Barley Soup

Nutritional information per serving:

Calories 119
Calories from fat 14%
Fat 2g
Saturated Fat 1g
Cholesterol 5mg
Sodium 428mg
Carbohydrate 20g
Dietary Fiber 5g
Sugars 4g
Protein 6g
Dietary Exchanges:
1 starch, 1 vegetable

Spicy Advice

For vegetarian option, omit bacon and use vegetable broth.

Italian Vegetable Soup ❄

Nutritional information per serving:

Calories 159
Calories from fat 18%
Fat 3g
Saturated Fat 1g
Cholesterol 6mg
Sodium 738mg
Carbohydrate 24g
Dietary Fiber 6g
Sugars 5g
Protein 10g
Dietary Exchanges:
1 starch, 1 vegetable,
1 lean meat

This minestrone style soup, hearty, healthy and satisfying, loaded with veggies and pasta, makes a delicious one-pot meal.

Makes 8 (1-cup) servings

1 tablespoon olive oil
1/2 cup coarsely chopped green pepper
1/2 cup coarsely chopped red onion
1/2 cup coarsely chopped celery
1 cup small zucchini chunks
2 ounces prosciutto, chopped
1 teaspoon minced garlic
1 cup peeled carrots, cut in small chunks or baby carrots
6 cups fat-free chicken broth or vegetable broth

1 (14 1/2-ounce) can diced tomatoes, drained
1 (15-ounce) can white navy beans, rinsed and drained
3/4 cup small penne pasta
1 teaspoon dried basil leaves
1 cup packed baby spinach leaves
Salt and pepper to taste
Grated Parmesan cheese, optional

Spicy Advice

When reheating, add more broth if too thick. For a vegetarian option, omit prosciutto and use vegetable broth.

1. In large nonstick pot coated with nonstick spray, heat olive oil and sauté green pepper, onion, and celery, about 5 minutes. Add zucchini, prosciutto, garlic and carrots; continue to sauté another 3-5 minutes or until tender.

2. Add broth, tomatoes, and beans; bring to boil. Add pasta and continue to cook 6-8 minutes or until pasta is tender. Add basil and spinach, stirring until spinach is wilted. Season to taste. Serve with Parmesan cheese, if desired.

Italian Vegetable Soup

Meatless Mediterranean Stew with Feta over Polenta

Eggplant, zucchini, red pepper, tomatoes and chickpeas sprinkled with feta makes a "wow" meatless one-dish meal. Polenta may be substituted with rice or couscous.

Makes 6 (1-cup) servings over polenta

1 tablespoon olive oil

2 cups chopped peeled eggplant

2 cups chopped zucchini

1 onion, chopped

1 red bell pepper, cored and chopped

1 teaspoon minced garlic

2 teaspoons dried oregano leaves

1 teaspoon paprika

1 (28-ounce) can diced tomatoes

1 (15-ounce) can chick peas, rinsed and drained

Salt and pepper to taste

1 (18-ounce) prepared polenta, cut into 8 slices

1/3 cup crumbled reduced-fat feta cheese

Spicy Advice

Look in the grocery for a roll of precooked polenta. Prepared polenta is easy to cook, and the buttery flavor perfectly contrasts the rich robust tomato vegetable mixture. Save extra polenta for another time.

1. In nonstick pot, heat oil and add eggplant, zucchini, onion and bell pepper. Cook until begins to soften, about 7 minutes. Add garlic, oregano, paprika, tomatoes and chick peas. Continue cooking until vegetables are tender. Season to taste.

2. Meanwhile, slice polenta and heat in nonstick skillet until begins to brown on one side, about 5 minutes; flip and cook until other side is brown, another 4 minutes. Polenta should be soft inside with lightly brown exterior.

3. To serve, place polenta on plate, top with stew and sprinkle with feta.

Meatless Mediterranean Stew with Feta over Polenta

Sweet Potato Chili over Couscous

**Nutritional information
per serving:**

Calories 312
Calories from fat 10%
Fat 3g
Saturated Fat 0g
Cholesterol 0mg
Sodium 626mg
Carbohydrate 61g
Dietary Fiber 11g
Sugars 12g
Protein 11g
Dietary Exchanges:
3 1/2 starch, 2 vegetable

This vegetarian entrée tops my list! The spicy chipotle chili powder, smoky tomatoes, and naturally sweet yams over unassuming couscous is fantastic.

Makes 6 (1-cup) servings with 1/2 cup couscous

1 tablespoon olive oil

1 onion, chopped

1 red bell pepper, cored and chopped

1 teaspoon minced garlic

1 tablespoon chili powder

1 teaspoon chipotle chili powder

1-1/2 pounds Louisiana yams (sweet potatoes), peeled and cut into 1/2-inch chunks (4 cups)

1 (14 1/2-ounce) can fire-roasted diced tomatoes

1 (15-ounce) can dark red kidney beans, rinsed and drained

1 1/2 cups vegetable broth

3 cups cooked couscous

1. In large nonstick pot, heat oil and sauté onion, bell pepper and garlic over medium heat until tender, about 5 minutes. Stir in chili and chipotle powder for 30 seconds. Add sweet potatoes, tomatoes, beans and broth.

2. Bring to boil, reduce heat, and cook about 20-30 minutes or until sweet potatoes are tender. Serve over couscous.

Spicy Advice

Chipotle chili powder has a smoky spicy flavor found in spice section. Fire-roasted tomatoes, also in groceries, have a smoky fiery flavor. Chili powder and diced tomatoes may be substituted to save a trip to the store.

Sweet Potato Chili ov

Roasted Vegetables with Pecans over Mixed Greens

Nutritional information per serving:

Calories 129
Calories from fat 59%
Fat 9g
Saturated Fat 1g
Cholesterol 0mg
Sodium 130mg
Carbohydrate 11g
Dietary Fiber 4g
Sugars 5g
Protein 4g
Dietary Exchanges:
2 vegetable, 2 fat

Roasting brings out the natural sweetness of this great assortment of veggies making this simple combination a snappy salad.

Makes 6 (3/4-cup) veggie servings over mixed greens

2 1/2 cups yellow squash, cut in 1 1/2-inch thick chunks (about 2 medium)

1 red onion, cut in chunks

2 cups 1-inch asparagus (about 1 pound)

1 (14-ounce) can artichoke hearts, drained and quartered

1/3 cup coarsely chopped pecans

2 tablespoons olive oil

Salt to taste

2- 3 teaspoons balsamic vinegar

4 cups mixed salad greens

Grated Parmesan cheese, optional

1. Preheat oven 450°F. Coat baking sheet with foil.

2. Toss squash, onion, asparagus, artichokes, and pecans in olive oil and salt to taste. Spread mixture in single layer on prepared pan.

3. Roast 15 minutes, stir, and continue roasting another 15 minutes or until lightly golden and browned. Drizzle with balsamic vinegar, stirring gently.

4. Serve vegetables over mixed greens. Sprinkle with Parmesan cheese, if desired.

Spicy Advice

Versatile and fantastic-serve as salad, over pasta, or as a side. Roasting simplifies cooking- toss in the oven and forget about it.

Roasted Vegetables with Pecans over Mixed Greens

Lentil Salad with Goat Cheese

Nutritional information per serving:

Calories 224
Calories from fat 29%
Fat 7g
Saturated Fat 4g
Cholesterol 15mg
Sodium 60mg
Carbohydrate 27g
Dietary Fiber 5g
Sugars 5g
Protein 15g
Dietary Exchanges:
1 1/2 starch, 1 vegetable,
1 1/2 lean meat

Light and refreshing, lentils are the base of this hearty salad packed with fresh ingredients. The touch of cloves adds spice, the mint invokes vibrancy and the light lemon dressing finishes it off!

Makes 6 cups

1 cup green or brown lentils, rinsed and drained

1/4 teaspoon ground cloves

1 cup chopped tomatoes

1/2 cup chopped celery

1/2 cup chopped green pepper

1/2 cup chopped onion

3 ounces goat cheese, crumbled

2 tablespoons chopped parsley

2 tablespoons chopped fresh mint

1/4 cup lemon juice

1 teaspoon honey

1 tablespoon olive oil

1/2 teaspoon minced garlic

Salt and pepper to taste

1. In medium nonstick pot, place lentils and cover with water 2 inches above lentils. Add cloves, and bring to boil. Reduce heat, cover, and simmer 20 minutes, or until lentils are tender. Drain, rinse with cold water. Cool.

2. In large bowl, combine tomatoes, celery, green pepper, onion, cheese, parsley, and mint. Stir in cooled lentils.

3. In small bowl, whisk together lemon juice, honey, oil, and garlic. Gently toss with salad and season to taste. Refrigerate.

Spicy Advice

Lentils, a member of the legume family, are inexpensive and very nutritious- high protein, good source of fiber and quick and easy to prepare.

Southwestern Tabbouleh

Nutritional information per serving:

Calories 172
Calories from fat 4%
Fat 1g
Saturated Fat 0g
Cholesterol 0mg
Sodium 180mg
Carbohydrate 36g
Dietary Fiber 9g
Sugars 3g
Protein 7g
Dietary Exchanges:
2 starch, 1 vegetable

Get familiar with bulgur — a high fiber nutty-tasting cracked wheat, prepared simply by adding hot water. Add this fantastic choice to your recipe repertoire.

Makes 8 servings

2 cups boiling water
1 1/2 cups cracked wheat (bulgur)
1 (15-ounce) can black beans, rinsed and drained
1 cup frozen corn, thawed
1 1/2 cups chopped tomatoes
1 bunch green onions, chopped

1 tablespoon minced cilantro
3 tablespoons orange juice
1/4 cup lemon juice
1/2 teaspoon ground cumin
1/2 teaspoon chili powder

1. In large bowl, pour boiling water over cracked wheat. Let set 45 minutes or until liquid is absorbed. Drain excess liquid.

2. In large bowl, combine cracked wheat, black beans, corn, tomatoes, green onions, and cilantro.

3. In small bowl, whisk together remaining ingredients. Toss with salad. Refrigerate.

Spicy Advice

Experiment with cracked wheat as a substitute for rice. Cracked wheat is found in health food stores or in groceries in Tabbouleh mixes; discard seasoning packet for this recipe.

Chocolate is derived from cocoa beans-if all beans are vegetables, **then chocolate must be a vegetable.**

Summertime Couscous

Nutritional information per serving:

Calories 215
Calories from fat 28%
Fat 7g
Saturated Fat 2g
Cholesterol 4mg
Sodium 187mg
Carbohydrate 31g
Dietary Fiber 3g
Sugars 3g
Protein 7g
Dietary Exchanges:
1 1/2 starch, 1 vegetable, 1 fat

A super summer dish highlighting garden ingredients. Give couscous a try — easy to make and just think of it as a rice replacement.

Makes 8 servings

1 3/4 cups boiling water or broth
1 1/2 cups couscous
1/2 cup chopped green onions
2 cups chopped tomatoes
1/2 cup chopped green pepper
1 1/2 cups finely chopped cucumber
1/2 cup finely chopped carrots
1/2 cup chopped fresh parsley,
 (flat leaf preferred)

1/2 cup chopped fresh mint
2/3 cup crumbled reduced-fat
 feta cheese
1/3 cup lemon juice
3 tablespoons olive oil
1 teaspoon minced garlic
Dash cayenne pepper
Salt and pepper to taste

1. In medium pot, bring water to boil. Stir in couscous, cover, and remove from heat; let stand 5-7 minutes. Transfer to large bowl and fluff with fork.

2. Add to couscous, green onions, tomatoes, green peppers, cucumber, carrot, parsley, mint and feta.

3. In small bowl, whisk together lemon juice, olive oil, garlic, cayenne, salt and pepper. Toss with salad. Refrigerate.

Summertime Couscous

Sweet Potato Salad

Always line a baking sheet with foil for easy clean-up.

A trendy and very tasty twist to potato salad featuring sweet potatoes with a hint of spice, toasty pecans, and tart cranberries in a maple citrus dressing.

Makes 10 (1/2-cup) servings

6 cups peeled Louisiana yams (sweet potatoes) chunks

1/2 teaspoon ground ginger

1/2 teaspoon ground cumin

3 tablespoons olive oil, divided

1/2 cup chopped green onions

1/4 cup dried cranberries

1/4 cup chopped pecans, toasted

2 tablespoons pure maple syrup

2 tablespoons orange juice

1 tablespoon lime juice

1/2 teaspoon ground nutmeg

1. Preheat oven 425°F. Line baking sheet with foil and coat with nonstick cooking spray.

2. On prepared pan, toss together potatoes with ginger, cumin and 1 tablespoon olive oil. Roast about 30 minutes or until potatoes are crisp. Cool and transfer to large bowl. Add green onions, cranberries and pecans.

3. In small bowl, whisk together maple syrup, orange and lime juice, nutmeg and remaining 2 tablespoons olive oil. Toss with potatoes. Serve or refrigerate.

Sweet Potato Salad

Baked Beans

Transform traditional baked beans into a spunky and special dish with lots of flavor. Can make earlier in the day, refrigerate — bring to room temperature about 30 minutes before baking.

Makes 6-8 servings

4 slices center cut bacon, chopped

2 onions, chopped

2 teaspoons minced garlic

1 cup beer

1 cup tomato sauce

1/4 cup light brown sugar

1/4 cup balsamic vinegar

2 tablespoons molasses

2 tablespoons Dijon mustard

3 (15-ounce) cans cannellini beans, rinsed and drained

Salt and pepper to taste

1. Preheat oven 350°F. Coat 2-quart casserole dish with nonstick cooking spray.

2. In large nonstick pot, cook bacon until crispy. Drain excess grease. Add onion and garlic, sauté 5-7 minutes or until tender. Add remaining ingredients, except beans, cook over medium heat 7 minutes.

3. Stir in beans, mixing well. Season to taste and transfer mixture into baking dish, bake 1 hour.

Spicy Advice

For vegetarian option, omit the bacon.

Butternut Squash Soufflé

Nutritional information per serving:

Calories 162
Calories from fat 9%
Fat 2g
Saturated Fat 0g
Cholesterol 53mg
Sodium 61mg
Carbohydrate 35g
Dietary Fiber 3g
Sugars 21g
Protein 4g
Dietary Exchanges:
1 1/2 starch, 1 other carbohydrate

Butternut squash has a sweet, nutty taste similar to pumpkin.

Had extra butternut squash and made this creamy yummy casserole.

Makes 4 (3/4-cup) servings

3 cups cubed peeled butternut squash	1/4 teaspoon ground nutmeg
1/4 cup sugar	1/2 teaspoon ground cinnamon
1/4 cup skim milk	1 egg
1 teaspoon vanilla extract	1/4 cup crushed honey nut toasted whole grain oat cereal
Salt to taste	1 tablespoon light brown sugar
1 tablespoon all-purpose flour	

1. Preheat oven 400°F. Coat 1-quart baking dish with nonstick cooking spray.

2. Place butternut squash in microwave-safe bowl with a little water, microwave until soft, 6-8 minutes. Drain and mash.

3. In prepared dish, combine mashed squash, sugar, milk, vanilla, salt, flour, nutmeg, cinnamon and egg, mixing well. Combine cereal and brown sugar. Sprinkle on top. Bake 20 minutes or until set.

Butternut Squash Soufflé

Cauliflower Crisp Stir-Fry

Cauliflower takes on a toasty rich flavor with few ingredients in this simple stir-fry. Try this once, and cauliflower will become a favorite veggie, yes, I am serious!

Makes 4 (3/4 cup) servings

2 tablespoons olive oil

4 cups cauliflower florets, cut into tiny pieces (trees)

Salt and pepper to taste

2 tablespoons grated Parmesan cheese

1. In large nonstick skillet, heat olive oil and add cauliflower, cook, stirring, 6-8 minutes, or until tender and crispy brown on edges.

2. Season to taste. Sprinkle with Parmesan cheese, serve.

Nutritional information per serving:

Calories 95
Calories from fat 67%
Fat 8g
Saturated Fat 1g
Cholesterol 2mg
Sodium 68mg
Carbohydrate 5g
Dietary Fiber 2g
Sugars 2g
Protein 3g
Dietary Exchanges:
1 vegetable, 1 1/2 fat

Marinated Asparagus

A splash of roasted garlic seasoned rice vinegar, dill, and orange give simple asparagus some spunk! Good served warm or chilled.

Makes 4 servings

2 tablespoons roasted garlic seasoned rice vinegar

2 tablespoons olive oil

1/2 teaspoon minced garlic

1 tablespoon fresh dill or 1 teaspoon dried dill weed leaves

1/2 teaspoon grated orange rind

Salt and pepper to taste

1 pound asparagus, cooked and cooled

1. In small bowl, whisk together all ingredients except asparagus. In shallow dish or resealable plastic bag, lay asparagus and cover with marinade.

2. Refrigerate in marinade to serve cold or serve with marinade for vegetable side.

Nutritional information per serving:

Calories 89
Calories from fat 64%
Fat 7g
Saturated Fat 1g
Cholesterol 0mg
Sodium 151mg
Carbohydrate 6g
Dietary Fiber 2g
Sugars 4g
Protein 3g
Dietary Exchanges:
1 vegetable, 1 1/2 fat

Tasty Kale and White Beans

Nutritional information per serving:

Calories 137
Calories from fat 21%
Fat 3g
Saturated Fat 1g
Cholesterol 4mg
Sodium 365mg
Carbohydrate 20g
Dietary Fiber 6g
Sugars 2g
Protein 8g
Dietary Exchanges:
1/2 starch, 2 vegetable,
1/2 lean meat

Kale, from the cabbage family, is very nutritious with powerful antioxidants.

Never cooked kale before? This recipe truly knocked it out of the park! One I will repeat many times.

Makes 6 servings

1/3 cup diced Canadian bacon

1 tablespoon olive oil

1 onion, chopped

1 pound kale, chopped (about 6 cups)

1 (15-ounce) can Great northern beans, rinsed and drained

1 cup fat-free chicken broth

Salt and pepper to taste

1. In large nonstick skillet coated with nonstick cooking spray over medium heat, cook Canadian bacon until turns golden brown, several minutes. Add oil and onion, sauté until tender, about 5 minutes.

2. Add kale, beans and broth and cook, stirring, about 10 minutes or until kale is tender. Season to taste.

Tasty Kale and White Beans

Mac and Cheese

Dark Roast

Rich and creamy with the different cheeses make this a top-notch mac and cheese. My daughter made this recipe for her college friends with rave reviews.

Makes 10-12 servings

1 (16-ounce) package whole wheat macaroni (or curly pasta)

1 tablespoon butter

1 onion, chopped

1/3 cup all-purpose flour

2 cups skim milk

2 cups fat-free half-and-half

1 tablespoon Dijon mustard

1/4 teaspoon dried thyme leaves

Salt and pepper to taste

1 1/4 cups shredded light Jarlsberg cheese (Swiss), divided

1 cup shredded white Cheddar cheese, divided

5 tablespoons grated Parmesan cheese, divided

3 tablespoons finely chopped parsley

1/4 cup bread crumbs

Spicy Advice

Great time to use whatever cheese you have in your refrigerator – toss it all in.

1. Preheat oven 350°F. Coat 3-quart oblong baking dish with nonstick cooking spray.

2. Cook macaroni according to package directions. Drain, set aside

3. In large nonstick pot, melt butter and sauté onion until tender, 5 minutes. Gradually stir in flour, stirring one minute. Gradually add milk and half-and-half, stirring constantly. Add mustard, thyme and season to taste.

4. Bring to boil, reduce heat, and cook 10 minutes, stirring, until mixture is thick and creamy. Stir in cheeses, reserving 2 tablespoons each cheese for topping. Combine cheese sauce with macaroni and transfer to prepared baking dish.

5. In small bowl, combine reserved cheese, parsley and bread crumbs. Sprinkle over macaroni. Bake 15-20 minutes or until cheese is melted and macaroni well heated.

Southwestern Rice

A meatless entrée or a hearty family pleasing side, this recipe is as simple as opening cans. Turn leftover rice into another recipe. Try using brown rice.

Makes 8 (1-cup) servings

2 cups cooked rice

1 (15-ounce) can corn, drained

1 (15-ounce) can black beans, rinsed and drained

1 (10-ounce) can tomatoes and green chilies

1 cup nonfat sour cream

2 cups shredded reduced-fat Mexican blend cheese, divided

1 bunch green onions, chopped (reserving 2 tablespoons)

1 (2 1/4-ounce) can sliced black olives, drained

1. Preheat oven 350°F. Coat 2-quart oblong baking dish with nonstick cooking spray.

2. Combine all ingredients using 1 3/4 cups cheese in prepared dish. Bake 45-50 minutes. Remove from oven and sprinkle with remaining 1/4 cup cheese and 2 tablespoons green onions. Return to oven 5 minutes or until cheese melted.

Nutritional information per serving:

Calories 269
Calories from fat 23%
Fat 7g
Saturated Fat 3g
Cholesterol 23mg
Sodium 720mg
Carbohydrate 38g
Dietary Fiber 5g
Sugars 5g
Protein 14g
Dietary Exchanges:
2 1/2 starch, 1 1/2 lean meat

Put mixture into a wrap for a mouthwatering meatless meal.

Southwestern Rice

Zucchini Au Gratin

Move over potatoes as garden fresh zucchini and fresh tomatoes baked in a white sauce topped with melted cheese makes a scrumptious au gratin.

Makes 6 servings

1 tablespoon butter

1 onion, coarsely chopped

2 pounds zucchini, sliced 1/4-inch thick (about 6 cups)

1 1/2 cups coarsely chopped tomatoes

Salt and pepper to taste

1/4 teaspoon ground nutmeg

2 tablespoons all-purpose flour

1 cup skim milk

1/2 cup fresh whole wheat bread crumbs or bread crumbs

1 cup reduced-fat shredded light Jarlsberg cheese (light Swiss cheese)

1. Preheat oven 350°F. Coat 10x7x2-inch baking dish with nonstick cooking spray.

2. In large nonstick skillet coated with nonstick cooking spray, melt butter, and cook onion over medium heat 5 minutes, stirring. Add zucchini, cook, covered, stirring occasionally, 10 minutes; add tomatoes cooking another 5 minutes. Season to taste and add nutmeg.

3. Stir in flour, and gradually add milk. Bring to boil, lower heat and cook, stirring, until thickened. Transfer to prepared dish.

4. In small bowl, combine bread crumbs and cheese, sprinkle on top zucchini mixture. Bake 15-20 minutes or until bubbly and cheese is melted.

Nutritional information per serving:

Calories 138
Calories from fat 31%
Fat 5g
Saturated Fat 2g
Cholesterol 10mg
Sodium 151mg
Carbohydrate 15g
Dietary Fiber 3g
Sugars 8g
Protein 11g
Dietary Exchanges:
1/2 starch, 2 vegetable, 1 lean meat

Spicy Advice

Tomatoes should be stored at room temperature to maximize flavor.

Baked Potato Casserole

Add crumbled bacon, if desired.

Turn those leftover baked or mashed potatoes into a delectable easy new side. A cross between mashed, au gratin and baked potato all in one.

Makes 8 servings

6 medium potatoes, baked	1 green bell pepper, cored and sliced
1/3 cup skim milk	1/2 teaspoon minced garlic
1 1/4 cups nonfat sour cream, divided	1 cup shredded reduced-fat Cheddar cheese
Season to taste	1/4 cup chopped green onion stems
1 onion, sliced	

1. Preheat oven 350°F. Coat 9x9x2-inch baking dish with nonstick cooking spray.

2. Mash potatoes with milk and 3/4 cup sour cream until creamy. Season to taste. Spread mashed potatoes in bottom of dish. Cover with remaining 1/2 cup sour cream.

3. In nonstick skillet, sauté onion, green pepper and garlic until tender, 5-7 minutes. Season to taste. Layer onion mixture over sour cream.

4. Sprinkle with cheese and green onions. Bake 25-30 minutes or until well heated.

Baked Potato Casserole

One Pot New Year's Day Meal

Medium Roast

Cabbage and black-eyed peas with meat and rice make this an ideal one-pot family meal for that lazy no-desire-to-cook day. And, it's really good!

Makes 8 (1-cup) servings

6 cups shredded cabbage

1 cup rice

1 pound ground sirloin

1 (10-ounce) diced tomatoes and green chilies

1 (14 1/2-ounce) can beef broth

1 (15-ounce) can black-eyed peas, rinsed and drained

Salt and pepper to taste

1. Preheat oven 350°F.

2. In large oven-proof pot, layer cabbage, rice, meat, tomatoes and green chilies, and beef broth.

3. Cook, covered, 1 hour 15 minutes, stirring after 40 minutes, until rice is tender and liquid absorbed. Stir in black-eyed peas and season to taste.

Nutritional information per serving:

Calories 212
Calories from fat 12%
Fat 3g
Saturated Fat 1g
Cholesterol 31mg
Sodium 446mg
Carbohydrate 30g
Dietary Fiber 3g
Sugars 2g
Protein 17g
Dietary Exchanges:
1 1/2 starch, 1 vegetable, 2 very lean meat

Chocolate-covered raisins, cherries, orange slices and strawberries all count as fruit, so who's counting.

Pineapple Zucchini Cake

Medium Roast

If you enjoy carrot cake, you will love this moist and delicious cake with a luscious cream cheese frosting. Does this cake count as a vegetable? I top with toasted pecans.

Makes 24 servings

Nutritional information per serving:

Calories 190
Calories from fat 34%
Fat 7g
Saturated Fat 3g
Cholesterol 27mg
Sodium 164mg
Carbohydrate 29g
Dietary Fiber 1g
Sugars 19g
Protein 3g
Dietary Exchanges:
2 other carbohydrate, 1 1/2 fat

2 cup all-purpose flour
3/4 cup sugar
1/3 cup flaked coconut
2 teaspoons baking soda
2 teaspoons ground cinnamon
3 tablespoons canola oil
2 eggs

1 teaspoon vanilla extract
2 cups shredded zucchini
1 (20-ounce) can crushed pineapple in juice, drained
1/2 cup chopped pecans
Cream Cheese Frosting (recipe follows)
Toasted pecans, optional

1. Preheat oven 350°F. Coat 13x9x2-inch pan with nonstick cooking spray.

2. In large bowl, combine flour, sugar, coconut, baking soda, and cinnamon.

3. In another bowl, combine oil, eggs, and vanilla; stir well. Stir egg mixture, zucchini, pineapple, and pecans into flour mixture. Batter will be stiff, mix well.

4. Transfer batter into prepared pan. Bake 25-30 minutes or until tooth pick inserted in center comes out almost clean. Cool and ice with Cream Cheese Frosting (see recipe). Top with toasted pecans, if desired.

Cream Cheese Frosting
The best icing!

2 tablespoons butter, softened
1 (8-ounce) package reduced-fat cream cheese

2 cups confectioners sugar
1 teaspoon vanilla extract

In mixing bowl, mix butter and cream cheese until smooth. Add confectioners sugar and vanilla, mixing until creamy.

Sweet Temptations

Birthdays are like chocolate chip cookies... there is no reason to think about how many we've had.

Chocolate Chip Oatmeal Cookies

Medium-Light Roast

Cookie craving? Can't decide between oatmeal and chocolate chip, this outrageous cookie gives you instant satisfaction for both. I don't even use a mixer.

Makes 3 dozen cookies

1/3 cup butter, softened
1/2 cup sugar
1/2 cup light brown sugar
1 egg
1 teaspoon vanilla extract
1 1/4 cups all-purpose flour

1/2 teaspoon baking powder
1/2 teaspoon baking soda
1 cup old-fashioned oatmeal
1/2 cup semi-sweet chocolate chips
1/2 cup chopped pecans, toasted

1. Preheat oven 350°F. Coat baking sheet with nonstick cooking spray.

2. In mixing bowl, mix together butter, sugar, and brown sugar until blended. Add egg and vanilla, mixing until creamy.

3. In another bowl, combine flour, baking powder and baking soda. Gradually add flour mixture to butter mixture, mixing only until combined. Stir in oatmeal, chocolate chips and pecans.

4. Drop dough by spoonfuls onto baking sheets. Bake 10-12 minutes or until cookie edges begin to brown.

You don't have to toast the pecans but toasting gives the pecans a wonderful toasty taste.

Chocolate Chip Oatmeal Cookies

German Chocolate Cookies

Espresso

Coconut, pecans, oatmeal and dark chocolate in a rich chocolate cookie just about covers my criteria for a bombshell cookie!

Makes 3 dozen

2 tablespoons butter
1/4 cup canola oil
3/4 cup light brown sugar
1 egg
1 teaspoon vanilla extract
1 teaspoon coconut extract
1 cup all-purpose flour

1/2 teaspoon baking soda
1/4 cup cocoa
1 cup old-fashioned oatmeal
1/3 cup flaked coconut
1/3 cup chopped pecans
1/3 cup dark chocolate chips

1. Preheat oven 350°F. Coat baking sheet with nonstick cooking spray.

2. In mixing bowl, beat together butter and oil. Add brown sugar, mixing until creamy. Add egg, vanilla and coconut extract, mixing well.

3. In small bowl, combine flour, baking soda, and cocoa. Add to creamed mixture, mixing well.

4. Stir in remaining ingredients. Drop by rounded teaspoons on baking sheet. Bake 8-10 minutes or until edges are just firm.

German Chocolate Cookies

Congo Bars

Growing up we adored Congo Bars, an indulgent blond brownie with butterscotch and chocolate chips, so here's my latest and greatest revision. Bart, my brother-in-law, insisted these were better than my original recipe — that's what I call good!

Makes 48 squares

Nutritional information
per serving:

Calories 106
Calories from fat 29%
Fat 3g
Saturated Fat 2g
Cholesterol 13mg
Sodium 55mg
Carbohydrate 18g
Dietary Fiber 0g
Sugars 13g
Protein 1g
Dietary Exchanges:
1 other carbohydrate, 1/2 fat

6 tablespoons butter, melted

2 cups dark brown sugar

2 eggs

1 teaspoon vanilla extract

2 1/2 cups all-purpose flour

2 teaspoons baking powder

1/2 teaspoon baking soda

1 cup buttermilk

1/2 cup dark chocolate chips

3/4 cup butterscotch chips

2/3 cup pecans, optional

1. Preheat oven 350°F. Coat 13x9x2-inch baking pan with nonstick cooking spray.

2. In large bowl, combine melted butter and brown sugar. Add eggs, one at a time, beating well and add vanilla.

3. In bowl, combine flour, baking powder and baking soda. Add buttermilk alternately with flour mixture, mixing well. Stir in chocolate chips, butterscotch chips, and pecans, if using.

4. Transfer to pan and bake 25-30 minutes or until toothpick inserted in center comes out clean. Don't overcook.

German Chocolate Cake Squares

German Chocolate Cake Squares

Dark Roast

German Chocolate Cake, one of my favorites, can be time consuming. Take a short cut with this awesome version featuring all the classic flavors without the fuss including a surprise bottom of coconut and pecans.

Makes 60-70 cake squares

2/3 cup chopped pecans
1/2 cup flaked coconut
1 (18.25-ounce) box German chocolate cake mix
1 1/3 cups water

1/3 cup canola oil
2 eggs
2 egg whites
Chocolate Icing (recipe follows)

1. Preheat oven 350°F. Coat 15x10x1-inch baking pan with nonstick cooking spray. Line pan with waxed paper and coat with nonstick cooking spray.

2. Sprinkle pecans and coconut evenly over paper. In mixing bowl, prepare cake mix with water, oil, eggs and egg whites according to directions on box. Spread batter carefully and evenly over pecans and coconut.

3. Bake 15-18 minutes or until top springs back when done. Cool and frost with Chocolate Icing (see recipe).

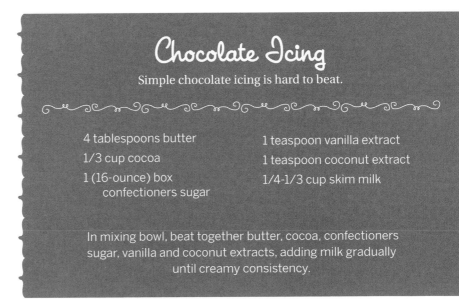

Chocolate Icing

Simple chocolate icing is hard to beat.

4 tablespoons butter
1/3 cup cocoa
1 (16-ounce) box confectioners sugar

1 teaspoon vanilla extract
1 teaspoon coconut extract
1/4-1/3 cup skim milk

In mixing bowl, beat together butter, cocoa, confectioners sugar, vanilla and coconut extracts, adding milk gradually until creamy consistency.

Chewy Pecan Bars

Flavored Coffee

Love pecan pie, well these easy-to-make bars taste like a buttery rich pecan pie!

Makes 48 squares

1 (18.25-ounce) box yellow
   cake mix

1/2 cup butter, melted

3 eggs, divided

1 cup dark corn syrup

1/4 cup light brown sugar

1 egg white

1 tablespoon vanilla extract

1 cup chopped pecans

1 Preheat oven 350°F. Coat 13x9x2-inch baking pan with nonstick cooking spray.

2 In mixing bowl, combine cake mix, melted butter and 1 egg, mixing until stiff dough forms. Press mixture evenly in bottom of prepared pan. Bake crust 15 minutes or until light brown.

3 In mixing bowl, combine remaining 2 eggs, corn syrup, brown sugar, egg white, and vanilla, mixing well. Stir in pecans. Pour evenly over baked crust and return to oven 20 minutes or until filling is set.

Chewy Pecan Bars

Orange Cupcakes with Citrus Cream Cheese Frosting

Medium-Dark
Roast

With cupcakes the fad, try this refreshing, light cupcake with a wonderful orange twist — sneak in whole wheat flour for a nutrition boost.

Makes 20-24 cupcakes

1 cup all-purpose flour

1 cup whole-wheat or all-purpose flour

1 teaspoon baking powder

1/2 teaspoon baking soda

1 teaspoon grated orange rind, optional

3/4 cup sugar

1/2 cup buttermilk

1 (12-ounce) can frozen orange juice
   concentrate, thawed and divided

1/3 cup canola oil

2 eggs

1 teaspoon vanilla extract

Citrus Cream Cheese Frosting
   (recipe follows)

1. Preheat oven 350°F. Line muffin tins with cupcake papers.

2. In medium bowl, combine both flours, baking powder, baking soda and orange rind.

3. In another bowl, combine sugar, buttermilk, orange juice concentrate (reserving 2 tablespoons), oil, eggs and vanilla. Whisk until well mixed.

4. Add sugar-buttermilk mixture to flour mixture, stirring only until blended. Divide batter among muffins, filling about half full. Bake 18-22 minutes or until tops spring back when lightly touched. Cool, frost with **Citrus Cream Cheese Frosting** (see recipe).

Citrus Cream Cheese Frosting

1 (8-ounce) package reduced-
   fat cream cheese

2 cups confectioners sugar

2 tablespoons frozen orange
   juice concentrate,
   reserved from above

In mixing bowl, beat together all ingredients
until creamy. Frost cupcakes.

Berry Good Oatmeal Cookie Cake

Medium-Dark
Roast

**Nutritional information
per serving:**

Calories 220
Calories from fat 36%
Fat 9g
Saturated Fat 5g
Cholesterol 36mg
Sodium 172mg
Carbohydrate 32g
Dietary Fiber 2g
Sugars 17g
Protein 4g
Dietary Exchanges:
2 other carbohydrate, 2 fat

A best ever luscious cookie cake picture perfect and perfect tasting.

Makes 12-16 servings

1/2 cup light brown sugar	2 tablespoons confectioners sugar
1 1/2 cups all-purpose flour	1/2 teaspoon almond extract
1 teaspoon baking soda	1/2 cup apricot preserves, divided
1 cup old-fashioned oatmeal	2 cups raspberries
1/2 cup butter, melted	2 cups sliced strawberries
1 teaspoon vanilla extract	1 cup blueberries
1 egg	1 tablespoon orange juice
6 ounces reduced-fat cream cheese	

1. Preheat oven 350°F. Coat 12-14-inch pizza pan with nonstick cooking spray.

2. In large bowl, combine brown sugar, flour, baking soda, and oatmeal. Add melted butter, vanilla, and egg, mixing well.

3. Press onto prepared pan, keeping dough 1-inch from edge of pan. Bake 10-12 minutes or until edges are set. Don't overbake. Cool.

4. In mixing bowl, beat together cream cheese, confectioners sugar, almond extract, and 1/4 cup apricot preserves until creamy. Spread on cooled crust and arrange fruit in design on pizza.

5. In microwave-safe dish, heat remaining 1/4 cup apricot preserves and orange juice, just until melted. Spoon glaze over fruit. Refrigerate until serving.

Berry Good Oatmeal Cookie Cake

Carrot Cake

Medium-Dark Roast

An incredibly moist and delicious three layer carrot cake with pineapple, pecans and coconut, and Cream Cheese Frosting. Best carrot cake ever!

Makes 16-20 servings

2 cups all-purpose flour	3/4 cup buttermilk
2 teaspoons baking soda	2 teaspoons vanilla extract
2 teaspoons ground cinnamon	2 cups grated carrots
2 eggs	1/2 cup flaked coconut
1 egg white	1 (8-ounce) can crushed pineapple
1/4 cup canola oil	1/2 cup chopped pecans
1 1/2 cups sugar	Cream Cheese Frosting (recipe follows)

1. Preheat oven 350°F. Coat three 9-inch round pans with nonstick cooking spray.

2. In bowl, mix together flour, baking soda and cinnamon; set aside.

3. In large mixing bowl, beat together eggs, egg white, oil, sugar, buttermilk, and vanilla. Gradually add flour mixture stirring until blended.

4. Stir in carrots, coconut, pineapple and pecans, mixing until combined. Pour batter into prepared pans. Bake 20-25 minutes or until tops spring back when lightly touched. Cool 10 minutes; then turn out onto racks to cool. Frost layers and sides with Cream Cheese Frosting (see recipe).

Spicy Advice

Just a little bit of orange rind adds a lot of flavor. Look for dried orange rind with spices.

Cream Cheese Frosting

What would Carrot Cake be without Cream Cheese Frosting?

1 (8-ounce) package reduced-fat cream cheese	1 teaspoon vanilla extract
3 tablespoons butter	1 (16-ounce) box confectioners sugar
1 teaspoon grated orange rind	

In mixing bowl, beat together cream cheese and butter until smooth. Add orange rind and vanilla, and gradually add confectioners sugar until creamy.

Quick Italian Cream Cake ❄️ 🥕

Nutritional information per serving:

Calories 305
Calories from fat 38%
Fat 13g
Saturated Fat 4g
Cholesterol 34mg
Sodium 240mg
Carbohydrate 45g
Dietary Fiber 0g
Sugars 35g
Protein 3g
Dietary Exchanges:
3 other carbohydrate, 2 1/2 fat

The ultimate short cut for my favorite cake begins with a cake mix! Best of all, everyone thought this "too good for words cake," was my recipe from scratch — your secret is safe.

Makes 16-20 servings

1 (18.25-ounce) box Butter Pecan Cake mix

1/3 cup canola oil

2 eggs

2 egg whites

1 1/4 cups water

1 teaspoon coconut extract

1/2 cup chopped pecans, toasted

1/2 cup flaked coconut

Cream Cheese Icing (recipe follows)

Toasted coconut and pecans, optional (about 2 tablespoons each)

1. Preheat oven 350°F. Coat three 9-inch pans with nonstick cooking spray.

2. In mixing bowl, beat together cake mix, oil, eggs, egg whites, water and coconut extract. Stir in pecans and coconut.

3. Pour batter evenly into prepared pans. Bake 12-15 minutes, until tops spring back when touched. Cool 10 minutes and turn out onto cooling racks. Frost layers and sides with Cream Cheese Icing (see recipe) and sprinkle with toasted coconut and pecans, if desired.

Cream Cheese Icing

The ultimate rich icing.

1 (8-ounce) package reduced-fat cream cheese

3 tablespoons butter

1 (16-ounce) box confectioners sugar

1 teaspoon vanilla extract

In mixing bowl, beat cream cheese and butter until smooth. Gradually add confectioners sugar, mixing until light. Add vanilla.

Quick Italian Cream Cake

Rich Chocolate Three Layer Cake with Chocolate Frosting

Rich Chocolate Three Layer Cake with Chocolate Frosting

Espresso

Nutritional information per serving:

Calories 313
Calories from fat 22%
Fat 8g
Saturated Fat 2g
Cholesterol 31mg
Sodium 141mg
Carbohydrate 57g
Dietary Fiber 1g
Sugars 44g
Protein 4g
Dietary Exchanges:
4 other carbohydrate, 1 1/2 fat

Ok chocoholics, I created this three layer very chocolaty rich, moist cake for my mother-in-law's birthday and this is truly a bite of chocolate decadence.

Makes 16-20 servings

1/3 cup canola oil

2 cups sugar

2 eggs

1 tablespoon vanilla extract

1 teaspoon butter extract

2 cups all-purpose flour

1/2 cup cocoa

1 1/2 teaspoons baking powder

1 teaspoon baking soda

1 cup nonfat sour cream

1 cup boiling water

Chocolate Frosting (recipe follows)

1. Preheat oven 350° F. Coat three 9-inch round pans with nonstick cooking spray.

2. In mixing bowl, beat together oil, sugar, eggs, vanilla and butter extracts.

3. In another bowl, combine flour, cocoa, baking powder and baking soda. Add to sugar mixture, alternately with sour cream, ending with flour mixture. Gradually add boiling water, mixing well. Transfer batter to prepared pans.

4. Bake 15-18 minutes or until top almost springs back, don't overbake. Ice with Chocolate Frosting (see recipe).

Chocolate Frosting

One of the best chocolate frostings to top the best chocolate cake.

4 tablespoons butter

2 ounces reduced-fat cream cheese

1 teaspoon vanilla extract

1/2 cup cocoa

1 (16-ounce) box confectioners sugar

4 tablespoons skim milk, as needed

In mixing bowl, beat together butter, cream cheese, and vanilla until creamy. Combine cocoa and confectioners sugar, and add to mixture gradually adding milk, until frosting is spreading consistency.

Chocolate Banana Bundt Cake

Nutritional information per serving:

Calories 188
Calories from fat 36%
Fat 8g
Saturated Fat 3g
Cholesterol 31mg
Sodium 283mg
Carbohydrate 26g
Dietary Fiber 1g
Sugars 16g
Protein 4g
Dietary Exchanges:
2 other carbohydrate,
1 1/2 fat

Thanks to an email from Stacy, I followed her suggested adaptation to my recipe and the outcome was a stupendous moist, rich, chocolate banana cake drizzled with Chocolate Icing. Best of all, few ingredients and easy!

Makes 16-20 servings

1 (18.25-ounce) box Devils Food Cake mix

1 (8-ounce) package reduced-fat cream cheese

1 cup mashed bananas (2 bananas)

2 eggs

1 1/3 cups water

1 1/2 teaspoons vanilla extract

1/2 cup chopped walnuts

Chocolate Glaze (recipe below), optional

Confectioners sugar, optional

1. Preheat oven 350°F. Coat 10-inch Bundt pan with nonstick cooking spray.

2. In large mixing bowl, beat together cake mix, cream cheese, bananas, eggs, water, and vanilla until well mixed. Stir in walnuts.

3. Transfer batter into prepared pan. Bake 40 minutes, or until inserted toothpick comes out clean. Do not overcook. Cool in pan 10 minutes, invert onto serving plate. If desired, drizzle with Chocolate Glaze (see recipe) and/or sprinkle with confectioners sugar.

Chocolate Glaze

The perfect finishing touch to this light chocolate cake.

1 tablespoon butter

1 tablespoon diet cola

2 teaspoons cocoa

1 teaspoon vanilla extract

1/3 cup confectioners sugar

In microwave-safe container, microwave butter, cola and cocoa about 1 minute or until boiling. Stir in vanilla and confectioners sugar, until smooth. If too thick, add little hot water.

White Chocolate Blueberry Bundt Cake

Medium-Dark Roast

Melt in your mouth decadence with two of my favorites, white chocolate and blueberries, with a perfectly matched Almond Glaze.

Makes 16-20 servings

1 cup white chocolate chips

6 tablespoons butter, softened

1 1/4 cups sugar

2 eggs

1 egg white

2 teaspoons vanilla extract

2 1/2 cups all-purpose flour

2 teaspoons baking powder

1 teaspoon baking soda

1 cup buttermilk

1/2 cup chopped pecans, optional

2 cups fresh or frozen blueberries

Almond Glaze (recipe follows)

1. Preheat oven 350°F. Coat Bundt pan with nonstick cooking spray.

2. In microwave-safe bowl, melt white chocolate chips in microwave 1 minute; stir until melted and cool slightly.

3. In mixing bowl, beat butter and sugar until creamy. Beat in eggs and egg white, one at a time, beating well after each addition. Add vanilla and melted white chocolate, mixing well.

4. In another bowl, combine flour, baking powder and baking soda. Gradually add flour mixture alternately with buttermilk just until combined. Add pecans, if desired. Pour half of batter into prepared pan.

5. Sprinkle blueberries over batter; top with remaining batter and swirl carefully with knife.

6. Bake 40-50 minutes or until toothpick inserted in cake comes out clean. Cool 10 minutes, invert on serving plate. Drizzle with Almond Glaze (see recipe).

Almond Glaze

Simple but makes a difference.

1 cup confectioners sugar

1 teaspoon almond extract

1 tablespoon skim milk

In small bowl, mix together all ingredients.

Easy Coconut Cake

White Chocolate Blueberry Bundt Cake

Easy Coconut Cake

Take a bite into coconut heaven with this undemanding, yet enticing mouth-watering coconut cake with the infamous cream cheese icing.

Makes 28 servings

Nutritional information per serving:

Calories 206
Calories from fat 31%
Fat 7g
Saturated Fat 2g
Cholesterol 16mg
Sodium 173mg
Carbohydrate 33g
Dietary Fiber 0g
Sugars 25g
Protein 3g
Dietary Exchanges:
2 other carbohydrate, 1 1/2 fat

1 (18.25-ounce) box white cake mix

1 egg

2 egg whites

1/4 cup canola oil

1 cup nonfat sour cream

1/2 cup non alcoholic Pina Colada mix

Cream Cheese Frosting (recipe follows)

2 tablespoons toasted coconut, optional

1. Preheat oven 350°F. Coat 13x9x2-inch pan with nonstick cooking spray.

2. In mixing bowl, combine cake mix, egg, egg whites, oil, sour cream, and Pina Colada mix, beating until well mixed. Transfer batter to prepared pan.

3. Bake 25 minutes or until toothpick inserted in center comes out clean. Cool and spread with Cream Cheese Frosting (see recipe) and sprinkle with toasted coconut, if desired.

Cream Cheese Frosting

Cream cheese, pecans, and coconut — is there anything better?

6 ounces reduced-fat cream cheese

2 tablespoons butter

1 (16-ounce) box confectioners sugar

1 teaspoon coconut extract

1 teaspoon vanilla extract

1/4 cup flaked coconut

1/3 cup chopped pecans, toasted

In mixing bowl, beat cream cheese and butter until creamy. Gradually add confectioners sugar, and coconut and vanilla extracts. Stir in coconut and pecans, spread on cooled cake.

Chocolate Cola Cake

I participated in a regional diet coke promotion and this recipe was all the rage each year so I am excited to share it with you.

Makes 60-70 squares

1/3 cup canola oil

1 3/4 cups sugar

1 egg

1 teaspoon vanilla extract

1 cup diet cola

1/2 cup buttermilk

2 cups all-purpose flour

1/4 cup cocoa

1 teaspoon baking soda

1 1/2 cups miniature marshmallows

Cola Chocolate Icing (recipe follows)

1. Preheat oven 350°F. Coat 15x10x1-inch pan with nonstick cooking spray.

2. In mixing bowl, beat together oil, sugar, egg and vanilla until creamy. In another bowl, mix together cola and buttermilk; set aside.

3. In small bowl, combine flour, cocoa, and baking soda; set aside. Add flour mixture to sugar mixture alternately with cola mixture, mixing only until just blended. Stir in miniature marshmallows.

4. Spread batter into prepared pan. Bake 12-15 minutes or until toothpick inserted in center comes out clean. Remove from oven, and immediately pour Cola Chocolate Icing (see recipe) on top of cake and carefully spread. Cool to room temperature, cut into squares.

Spicy Advice

For cakes like squares, make in 13x9x2-inch pan, bake 30-35 minutes.

Cola Chocolate Icing

This icing hardens on cake-delicious.

6 tablespoons butter

1/3 cup diet cola

1/4 cup cocoa

1 (16-ounce) box confectioners sugar

1 teaspoon vanilla extract

In medium pot, combine butter, cola, and cocoa, bring to boil. Remove from heat, and add confectioners sugar and vanilla, mixing until smooth. Icing will thicken.

Gingerbread with Cinnamon Pecan Crumble

Flavored
Coffee

**Nutritional information
per serving:**

Calories 247
Calories from fat 33%
Fat 9g
Saturated Fat 3g
Cholesterol 23mg
Sodium 126mg
Carbohydrate 39g
Dietary Fiber 1g
Sugars 21g
Protein 3g
Dietary Exchanges:
2 1/2 other carbohydrate, 2 fat

I promised my sister, Ilene, not another book without a gingerbread recipe and this fabulous recipe with a crumble topping was unanimously declared — the best gingerbread ever!

Makes 16 servings

1/4 cup butter, softened

1/4 cup canola oil

1/3 cup sugar

1 cup molasses

1 egg

1 tablespoon vanilla extract

2 cups all-purpose flour

1 teaspoon baking soda

1 teaspoon ground ginger

1 teaspoon ground cinnamon

1/2 cup buttermilk

1/4 cup hot water

Cinnamon Pecan Crumble
(recipe follows)

1. Preheat oven 325°F. Coat 9x9x2-inch square baking pan with nonstick cooking spray.

2. In mixing bowl, mix butter, oil, sugar, molasses, egg and vanilla until creamy. In another bowl, combine flour, baking soda, ginger, and cinnamon; add alternately to butter mixture with buttermilk and water, beating well. Transfer to prepared pan and sprinkle with Cinnamon Pecan Crumble (see recipe).

3. Bake 40-50 minutes, or until toothpick inserted into center of cake comes out clean. Don't overcook.

Cinnamon Pecan Crumble

Yummy!

1/3 cup light brown sugar

2 teaspoons ground cinnamon

1/4 cup all-purpose flour

1 tablespoon butter, melted

1 teaspoon vanilla extract

1/3 cup chopped pecans

In small bowl, mix together all ingredients with fork until crumbly.

Chocolate Silk Cheesecake

Dark Roast

A rich mousse-like chocolate cheesecake. Surprise, I boosted the nutrition by using tofu, giving the recipe a light creamier consistency, with monumental flavor. Serve with fresh berries.

Makes 12-16 servings

1 cup chocolate sandwich cookie crumbs

2 tablespoons butter, melted

1 teaspoon plus 1 tablespoon vanilla extract, divided

2 (8-ounce) packages reduced-fat cream cheese

1 (12-ounce) package soft tofu

1 cup sugar

2 eggs

3 egg whites

3 tablespoons cocoa

1 tablespoon all-purpose flour

1. Preheat oven 350°F. Coat 9-inch spring form pan with nonstick cooking spray.

2. In small bowl, combine cookie crumbs, butter, and 1 teaspoon vanilla, mixing with fork. Press into bottom of prepared pan.

3. In mixing bowl, beat cream cheese, tofu and sugar until light. Add eggs and egg whites, one at a time, mixing until creamy. Add cocoa, flour, and remaining 1 tablespoon vanilla, mixing well.

4. Pour into prepared crust and bake 55-60 minutes or until filling is set. Cool on wire rack and refrigerate until well chilled.

Chocolate Silk Cheesecake

Heavenly Yam Delight

An exceptionally delicious and light make-ahead dessert with yummy layers of yam-cinnamon, cream cheese filling and whipped topping. Don't let this combination fool you, as it will surprisingly tantalize your taste buds.

Makes 16 servings

1 cup all-purpose flour

1/4 cup plus 2/3 cup confectioners sugar, divided

1/3 cup chopped pecans

6 tablespoons butter, softened

1 (8-ounce) package reduced-fat cream cheese

1 (8-ounce) container fat-free frozen whipped topping, thawed, divided

1 (29-ounce) can sweet potatoes (Louisiana yams), drained

1/2 teaspoon ground cinnamon

1/4 cup sugar

1 Preheat oven 350°F. Coat 13x9x2-inch pan with nonstick cooking spray.

2 In large bowl, combine flour, 1/4 cup confectioners sugar, pecans, and butter. Press into bottom of pan. Bake 20 minutes. Set aside to cool.

3 In mixing bowl, mix cream cheese and remaining 2/3 cup confectioners sugar until creamy. Fold in 3/4 cup whipped topping. Carefully spread cream cheese mixture over cooled crust.

4 In mixing bowl, beat sweet potatoes, cinnamon, and sugar until smooth. Carefully spread over cream cheese mixture. Top with remaining whipped topping. Refrigerate.

Spicy Advice

Fresh cooked sweet potatoes may be used. 1 cooked sweet potato= 1 cup mashed (need 2 cups for this recipe). Toast the pecans for added flavor.

A balanced diet is a
cookie in both hands.

Strawberry Meringue Dessert

A divine irresistible light refreshing strawberry dessert.

Makes 12 servings

1 1/2 cups graham cracker crumbs

8 tablespoons sugar, divided

1/4 cup butter, melted

4 egg whites

1 teaspoon vanilla extract

1 quart fresh strawberries, hulled and sliced

1 (8-ounce) container frozen fat-free whipped topping, thawed

1. Preheat oven 350°F. Coat 9x9x2-inch baking pan with nonstick cooking spray.

2. In bowl, combine crumbs, 2 tablespoons sugar, and melted butter. Stir until well blended and press into prepared pan.

3. In mixing bowl, beat egg whites until soft peaks form. Gradually add 4 tablespoons sugar, beating until stiff peaks form. Add vanilla. Carefully spread meringue over crumb layer. Bake 15 minutes; cool completely.

4. In another bowl, sprinkle strawberries with remaining 2 tablespoons sugar. Let stand 15 minutes; drain. Spread whipped topping over cooled meringue and top with strawberries. Refrigerate.

Fresh Strawberry Pie

Medium-Dark Roast

In minutes, whip up this simple luscious strawberry pie.

Makes 8 servings

1 (9-inch) pie crust

1 cup water

2 heaping tablespoons cornstarch

2/3 cup sugar

2/3 (3-ounce) package lemon gelatin

2 cups fresh sliced strawberries

1. Bake pie crust according to directions. Cool

2. In small nonstick pot, combine water, cornstarch and sugar. Bring to boil, stirring, reduce heat and cook until thickened and bubbly.

3. Remove from heat, stir in lemon gelatin. Add strawberries and pour into baked pie shell. Refrigerate at least 3-4 hours before serving.

Passport Pleasures

A vacation is like a diet,
it has a beginning and ending.

Asian Sliders with Pineapple Salsa ❄

Nutritional information per serving:

Calories 160
Calories from fat 23%
Fat 4g
Saturated Fat 1g
Cholesterol 46mg
Sodium 184mg
Carbohydrate 20g
Dietary Fiber 1g
Sugars 8g
Protein 11g
Dietary Exchanges:
1 1/2 starch, 1 lean meat

Outrageously out of this world. Burgers bursting with Asian flavors topped with pineapple salsa served in miniature buns make the ultimate pick-up. Can make burgers earlier in the day, refrigerate, and cook when ready to serve. Great served at room temperature.

Makes 24 sliders

1 3/4 pounds ground sirloin

1/3 cup panko bread crumbs

1/3 cup chopped green onions

1 teaspoon ground ginger

2 teaspoons minced garlic

2 egg whites

6 tablespoons hoisin sauce, divided

24 miniature rolls (Hawaiian bread)

Pineapple Salsa (recipe below)

1. Preheat oven 450°F. Line baking sheet with foil.

2. In large bowl, combine all ingredients except rolls using 4 tablespoons hoisin sauce. Form into miniature patties (heaping tablespoons depending on size of bun) and place on prepared pan.

3. Brush tops of burgers with remaining 2 tablespoons hoisin sauce. Bake 10-12 minutes or until done. Slit rolls and place burger with about a tablespoon Pineapple Salsa (see recipe).

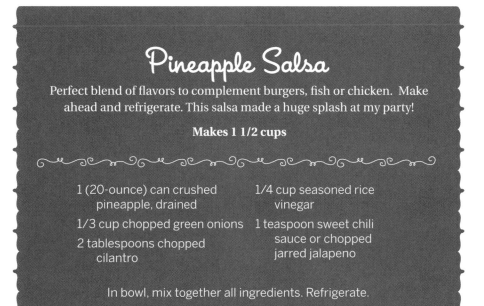

Pineapple Salsa

Perfect blend of flavors to complement burgers, fish or chicken. Make ahead and refrigerate. This salsa made a huge splash at my party!

Makes 1 1/2 cups

1 (20-ounce) can crushed pineapple, drained

1/3 cup chopped green onions

2 tablespoons chopped cilantro

1/4 cup seasoned rice vinegar

1 teaspoon sweet chili sauce or chopped jarred jalapeno

In bowl, mix together all ingredients. Refrigerate.

Asian Sliders with Pineapple Salsa

Mandarin Steak Salad with Ginger Vinaigrette

Medium Roast

Nutritional information (without vinaigrette) per serving:

Calories 274
Calories from fat 33%
Fat 10g
Saturated Fat 3g
Cholesterol 55mg
Sodium 90mg
Carbohydrate 16g
Dietary Fiber 6g
Sugars 9g
Protein 29g
Dietary Exchanges:
2 vegetable, 1/2 fruit,
3 lean meat

Steak, oranges, peppers and peanuts on mixed greens with a zingy vinaigrette makes an unbeatable entree salad.

Makes 4 servings

1 (16-ounce) sirloin steak, trimmed of fat

Orange Marinade (see recipe)

8 cups mixed greens

1 (11-ounce) can mandarin oranges, drained

1 red bell pepper, cored and thinly sliced

1 bunch green onions, chopped

1/3 cup chopped peanuts

Ginger Vinaigrette (see recipe)

1. Marinate steak in Orange Marinade (see recipe). Refrigerate 2 hours or overnight. Remove steak from marinade. In large nonstick skillet over medium heat, sear meat cooked to preference. Remove from skillet; slice and set aside.

2. Place mixed greens on plate, and top with mandarin oranges, red pepper, green onions, and sliced seared steak. Sprinkle with peanuts, serve with Ginger Vinaigrette (recipe follows).

Spicy Advice

Unpeeled fresh ginger will keep three weeks in the refrigerator.

Orange Marinade

An Asian infused marinade.

2 tablespoons orange marmalade

1 teaspoon minced fresh ginger

1 teaspoon minced garlic

2 tablespoons lemon juice

2 tablespoons seasoned rice vinegar

2 tablespoons orange juice

1 teaspoon olive oil

In plastic resealable bag,
mix together all ingredients. Add steak,
refrigerate two hours or overnight.

Ginger Vinaigrette

Ever tasted a vinaigrette you
wished you had the recipe - well, you have it!

Makes 3/4 cup

1 teaspoon minced fresh ginger

2 tablespoons olive oil

1 tablespoon dark sesame oil

1/2 cup seasoned rice wine vinegar

In small bowl, whisk together all ingredients.

Mandarin Steak Salad with Ginger Vinaigrette

Asian Cucumber Salad

The citrus and ginger-soy sauce dressing turn cucumbers, tomatoes and avocados into a splendid salad.

Makes 4 (3/4 cup) servings

2 large cucumbers

1/2 cup chopped avocado

1/2 cup chopped tomatoes

2 tablespoons low-sodium soy sauce

2 tablespoons seasoned rice vinegar

2 tablespoon orange juice

1 tablespoon lemon juice

1 teaspoon grated fresh ginger

1 teaspoon sesame seeds, toasted

1. Partially peel (peel in strips lengthwise) cucumbers, cut in half lengthwise; remove seeds by scraping with spoon and cut into thin slices horizontally (instead of chopping), about 2 cups sliced.

2. In bowl, place cucumbers, avocado and tomatoes. In small bowl, whisk together soy sauce, vinegar, orange and lemon juice, and ginger. Toss with cucumber mixture.

3. Sprinkle with sesame seeds, serve.

Spicy Advice

To easily remove seeds from cucumber: Cut in half lengthwise and run spoon down center of cucumber half to scoop out seeds.

Asian Cucumber Salad

Oriental Pasta Salad

Medium Roast

Flavors, crunch, and texture meld together for a pasta salad surprise. This fantastic combination makes a fulfilling vegetarian entrée (with edamame for a dose of protein) or a super salad side, ranking high on my list.

Make 8 (1 cup) servings

1 (8-ounce) package bowtie pasta

1 (3-ounce) package Oriental flavor Ramen noodle soup mix

1/3 cup sliced almonds

2 cups coleslaw mix (shredded cabbage)

1 cup shelled edamame, cooked according to package directions

1/2 cup chopped green onions

1 (15-ounce) can mandarin oranges, drained

3 tablespoons sugar

2 tablespoons olive oil

1/4 cup seasoned rice vinegar

1 tablespoon low-sodium soy sauce

1. Preheat oven 350°F.

2. Cook pasta according to package directions. Drain, cool.

3. Combine Ramen noodles (set seasoning packet aside) and almonds on baking sheet; bake 5-7 minutes or until light brown. Set aside, cool.

4. In large bowl, combine pasta, coleslaw, edamame, green onions, and mandarin oranges.

5. In another small bowl, whisk together seasoning packet, sugar, olive oil, vinegar and soy sauce. When ready to serve, toss pasta mixture with dressing, and then add browned noodles and almonds.

Spicy Advice

Make everything ahead of time (cook pasta, brown noodles, make dressing) and toss together when ready to serve.

If we're going to get bags as we get older, **they might as well be bags we use to travel.**

Southwestern Sweet Potato Salad

Nutritional information per serving:

Calories 113
Calories from fat 28%
Fat 4g
Saturated Fat 0g
Cholesterol 0mg
Sodium 99mg
Carbohydrate 19g
Dietary Fiber 3g
Sugars 4g
Protein 2g
Dietary Exchanges:
1 1/2 starch, 1/2 fat

Sensational! This combination of roasted sweet yams, crunchy corn, black beans in a light jalapeno dressing — an explosion of flavors and colors.

Makes 12 (1/2-cup) servings

6 cups peeled sweet potato (Louisiana yams) chunks (about 2 1/2 pounds)

Salt and pepper to taste

3 tablespoons olive oil, divided

1/2 cup chopped red bell pepper

1/2 cup chopped red onion

2/3 cup frozen corn, thawed

2/3 cup black beans, drained and rinsed

1/4 cup chopped cilantro

3 tablespoons lime juice

1 teaspoon minced garlic

1 tablespoon jarred jalapeno slices

1. Preheat oven 425°F. Coat foil lined baking sheet with nonstick cooking spray.

2. On prepared pan, toss together sweet potatoes, salt and pepper and 1 tablespoon olive oil. Roast about 30 minutes or until potatoes are crisp. Cool.

3. In large bowl, combine sweet potatoes, red bell pepper, red onion, corn, black beans and cilantro.

4. In blender, puree lime juice, garlic, jalapeno and remaining 2 tablespoons olive oil. Toss with potato mixture and serve.

Southwestern Sweet Potato Salad

Coconut Shrimp with Asian Greens

Shrimp perk up with a crispy Panko bread crumb-coconut coating, infused in an Asian marinade, and oven-baked for easy clean-up.

Makes 6 servings

2 tablespoons honey	1/2 cup flaked coconut
1 tablespoon lemon juice	1/3 cup cornstarch
1 teaspoon minced garlic	Salt and pepper to taste
1 tablespoon minced fresh ginger	3 egg whites, lightly beaten
1 1/2 pounds peeled shrimp	Asian Greens (see recipe)
1 cup panko bread crumbs	

1. In resealable plastic bag, combine honey, lemon juice, garlic, and ginger. Add shrimp, refrigerate one hour (time permitting) or until ready to cook.

2. Preheat oven 425°F. Line baking sheet with foil; coat with nonstick cooking spray.

3. In food processor, pulse bread crumbs and coconut until fine crumbs and place on plate. In shallow bowl, combine cornstarch and season to taste. In another bowl, place egg whites.

4. Coat shrimp with cornstarch, dip into egg whites, and roll in coconut mixture. Place shrimp on prepared pan. Bake 15-20 minutes or until shrimp are done. Serve on Asian Greens (recipe follows).

Nutritional information per serving:

Calories 388
Calories from fat 47%
Fat 20g
Saturated Fat 4g
Cholesterol 55mg
Sodium 684mg
Carbohydrate 23g
Dietary Fiber 6g
Sugars 15g
Protein 29g
Dietary Exchanges:
2 vegetable, 1 other carbohydrate, 3 lean meat, 2 fat

Spicy Advice

You can use this shrimp as an entree or to top any salad.

Asian Greens

Serve this super salad alone, with shrimp or chicken.

1 (3-ounce) package Ramen noodles, broken up, discard seasoning packet	1 cucumber, peeled and sliced
1/2 cup sliced almonds	1 red bell pepper, cored and cut into thin strips
4 cups shredded Napa cabbage	1 bunch green onions, chopped
4 cups baby spinach	

1. In nonstick skillet coated with nonstick cooking spray, cook noodles and almonds over medium heat, stirring, until golden brown. Watch carefully. Cool

2. When ready to serve toss all ingredients together with your favorite dressing.

Nutritional information per serving:

Calories 322
Calories from fat 27%
Fat 10g
Saturated Fat 4g
Cholesterol 168mg
Sodium 333mg
Carbohydrate 33g
Dietary Fiber 5g
Sugars 6g
Protein 25g
Dietary Exchanges:
2 starch, 1 vegetable, 3 lean meat

Thai Shrimp

Dark Roast

Introduce yourself to popular Thai cuisine with an easy shrimp and pasta recipe with an alluring mild sauce of garlic, ginger, peanut butter, and peanuts.

Makes 4 servings

1 1/2 cups fat-free chicken broth

1 tablespoon low-sodium soy sauce

1 tablespoon plus 1 teaspoon peanut butter

2 teaspoons sesame or sesame chili oil

1 green bell pepper, cored and diced

1 teaspoon minced garlic

1 tablespoon minced fresh ginger

1 pound medium shrimp, peeled

1 (8-ounce) package vermicelli

2 tablespoons dry roasted chopped peanuts

1/4 cup chopped green onions

1. In small nonstick pot, combine broth, soy sauce, peanut butter, and sesame oil. Whisk until blended. Bring to boil, reduce heat, and cook 5 minutes; set aside.

2. In large nonstick skillet coated with nonstick cooking spray, sauté green pepper, garlic and ginger over medium heat 3 minutes. Add shrimp, cook several minutes. Add reserved soy broth sauce to shrimp, continue cooking until shrimp are done, 3-5 minutes.

3. Cook pasta according to package directions. Drain; toss with shrimp mixture. Sprinkle with peanuts and green onions.

Thai Shrimp

Greek Shrimp

Grab a large skillet for a quick journey to the Mediterranean. Take advantage of the sumptuous sauce. Serve with pasta or rice (try whole grain pasta or brown rice).

Makes 6-8 servings

Nutritional information per serving:

Calories 182
Calories from fat 32%
Fat 6g
Saturated Fat 1g
Cholesterol 170mg
Sodium 567mg
Carbohydrate 9g
Dietary Fiber 2g
Sugars 4g
Protein 21g
Dietary Exchanges:
2 vegetable,
3 lean meat

2 tablespoons olive oil

1 onion, chopped

1 (28-ounce) can diced tomatoes

1/2 cup chopped parsley

1 tablespoon minced garlic

1 tablespoon dried oregano leaves

Salt and pepper to taste

2 pounds medium shrimp, peeled

1/4 cup sliced Kalamata olives

1 cup frozen peas, thawed

1/3 cup crumbled reduced-fat feta cheese

1. In large nonstick skillet over medium heat, heat olive oil and sauté onion until tender. Stir in tomatoes, parsley, garlic, oregano, and season to taste. Bring to boil, reduce heat, cover, and cook 15 minutes, stirring occasionally.

2. Add shrimp and olives; continue cooking until shrimp are done, about 5-7 minutes. Add peas, cook several minutes. Sprinkle with feta, serve.

Greek Shrimp

Mediterranean Chicken Summer Stir-Fry

Nutritional information per serving:

Calories 183
Calories from fat 32%
Fat 7g
Saturated Fat 1g
Cholesterol 51mg
Sodium 203mg
Carbohydrate 9g
Dietary Fiber 3g
Sugars 5g
Protein 23g
Dietary Exchanges:
2 vegetable, 2 1/2 lean meat

Came home, poured myself a glass of wine, cut up everything, and threw this summer sensation together in 20 minutes for a scrumptious stir-fry. I served it over angel hair pasta.

Makes 8 (1 cup) servings

1 1/2 pounds boneless, skinless chicken breasts, cut into 1-inch slices

3 teaspoons dried oregano leaves, divided

Salt and pepper to taste

2 tablespoons olive oil

4 cups diced yellow squash (about 2 large)

4 cups diced zucchini (about 2 large)

1 onion, diced

2 tablespoons lemon juice

1 pint grape tomatoes, halved

1/4 cup sliced Kalamata olives

1/4 cup chopped fresh parsley

1/4 cup crumbled reduced-fat feta cheese

1. Season chicken with 2 teaspoons oregano, and season to taste.

2. In large nonstick skillet, heat olive oil and cook chicken 3 minutes, stirring, or until chicken starts to brown. Add squash, zucchini, and onion, stirring, and continue cooking 5 minutes.

3. Add lemon juice, tomatoes, olives and remaining 1 teaspoon oregano, cooking another 5 minutes or until chicken is done and vegetables are tender. Add parsley, cooking one minute. Sprinkle with feta, serve.

Spicy Advice

Turn into a summer vegetarian dish without the chicken or use shrimp for a seafood variation. However you prepare it, these bold flavors make a wonderful combination.

I feel about airplanes the way I feel about diets. It seems to me that they are wonderful things for other people to go on.

Chicken Tuscan Primavera

Medium Roast

With chicken, mushrooms, sun-dried tomatoes, artichokes, basil, spinach and wine, this world-winning dish is reminiscent of a light and fulfilling Italian meal.

Makes 4-6 servings

Nutritional information per serving:

Calories 443
Calories from fat 15%
Fat 7g
Saturated Fat 1g
Cholesterol 66mg
Sodium 237mg
Carbohydrate 51g
Dietary Fiber 3g
Sugars 5g
Protein 37g
Dietary Exchanges:
3 starch, 1 vegetable,
3 lean meat

1 (12-ounce) package fetttuccine

2 tablespoons olive oil

1 1/2 pounds skinless, boneless chicken breasts, cut into chunks or strips

1 teaspoon minced garlic

1/2 pound fresh mushrooms, sliced

1 onion, chopped

1 teaspoon dried basil leaves

1/2 cup chopped or sliced sun-dried tomatoes, reconstituted

1 (14-ounce) can artichoke quarters, drained

1/2 cup fat-free chicken broth

1 cup white wine or cooking wine

1 cup packed baby spinach

Salt and pepper to taste

2 ounces mozzarella cheese (fresh preferred), cut into pieces

2 tablespoons pine nuts, toasted

1. Cook fettuccine according to package directions, drain. Set aside.

2. In large nonstick skillet, heat olive oil and cook chicken over medium high heat until lightly brown. Add garlic, mushrooms, and onion sautéing until tender.

3. Add basil, sun-dried tomatoes, artichokes, broth and wine, bring to boil, cook 5 minutes or until chicken is done. Add spinach, and cook until wilted. Season to taste.

4. Add pasta and toss together. If desired, add mozzarella and sprinkle with pine nuts, serve.

Chicken Tikka Masala

When a friend requested this recipe, I decided to make an everyday kitchen friendly version with no long list of new intimidating spices. Indian inspired but known in Britain as a national favorite, the chicken, tender and flavorful, with the yogurt marinade and sauce is richly spiced with a hint of sweetness.

Makes 8 servings

Nutritional information per serving:

Calories 195
Calories from fat 15%
Fat 3g
Saturated Fat 1g
Cholesterol 66mg
Sodium 546mg
Carbohydrate 12g
Dietary Fiber 0g
Sugars 7g
Protein 30g
Dietary Exchanges:
1 vegetable, 1/2 fat-free milk, 3 very lean meat

1 cup nonfat plain yogurt

1 tablespoon lemon juice

2 teaspoons ground cumin

1 teaspoon ground cinnamon

1 teaspoon cayenne pepper

1 tablespoon plus 1 teaspoon grated fresh ginger, divided

2 teaspoons minced garlic, divided

2 pounds skinless, boneless chicken breasts

1 tablespoon canola oil

1 onion, finely chopped

1 (28-ounce) can diced tomatoes with juice

1 (8-ounce) can tomato sauce

Pinch sugar

1 cup nonfat half-and-half

Salt and pepper to taste

1/4 cup chopped fresh cilantro leaves, optional

Spicy Advice

Serve with Garlic Fried Rice (page 221)

1. In resealable plastic bag or shallow glass dish, combine yogurt, lemon juice, cumin, cinnamon, cayenne, 1 tablespoon ginger, 1 teaspoon minced garlic and chicken. Refrigerate overnight or minimum 1 hour.

2. Preheat broiler. Remove chicken from refrigerator, place on foiled lined baking sheet. Discard extra yogurt mixture. Broil chicken 20 minutes, turn over, and continue cooking another 15 minutes or until chicken is done depending on size of chicken breasts. (Chicken should be lightly charred in spots)

3. Meanwhile, in large nonstick skillet, heat oil, and sauté onion until golden, stirring, 7 minutes. Add remaining 1 teaspoon ginger, 1 teaspoon garlic, diced tomatoes, tomato sauce, and pinch of sugar. Bring to boil, reduce heat, and cook, covered, 15 minutes, stirring occasionally.

4. Stir in half-and-half, cooking until well heated.

5. When chicken is done, cut into 1-inch chunks and add to sauce mixture. Heat well and season to taste. Before serving, sprinkle with cilantro, if desired.

Jamaican Jerk Chicken Kabobs

Dark Roast

Zingy and gingery flavors meld together creating this enticing, exciting shish kabob. Sweet pineapple, mellow mushrooms and colorful peppers perfectly complement the spicy chicken. Include your choice of fruit and veggies on the kabobs.

Makes 6 servings

2 green onions, chopped

1 jalapeno pepper, seeded and coarsely chopped

1 tablespoon minced fresh ginger

2 tablespoons seasoned rice vinegar

2 tablespoons Worcestershire sauce

1 teaspoon olive oil

1 teaspoon ground allspice

1 teaspoon dried thyme leaves

Salt and pepper to taste

1 1/2 pound skinless, boneless chicken breast chunks

1 red pepper, cut into 1-inch pieces

1 green pepper, cut into 1-inch pieces

1/2 pound small mushrooms

1 pineapple, cut into chunks

1. In blender or food processor, process green onions, jalapeno, ginger, vinegar, Worcestersauce, olive oil, allspice, thyme, and season to taste until mixed.

2. In resealable plastic bag or glass dish, combine green onion mixture and chicken, coating well. Refrigerate one hour.

3. Divide marinated chicken, peppers, mushrooms and pineapple and place onto kabobs. Discard marinade.

4. Preheat broiler. Place kabobs on foil lined pan. Broil 5 – 7 minutes. Turn and continue to broil another 5-7 minutes or until chicken is done. Shish kabobs may be grilled.

Spicy Advice

Try using roasted garlic or red pepper seasoned rice vinegar for easy extra flavor.

I don't think America will have really made it until we have our own salad dressing. *Until then we're stuck behind the French, Italians, Russians and Caesarians.*

Great Greek Meatballs with Orzo

Nothing beats meatballs and spaghetti until you try these incredible Mediterranean meatballs in this time-saver Marinara sauce.

Makes 6 servings

Nutritional information per serving:

Calories 464
Calories from fat 19%
Fat 9g
Saturated Fat 3g
Cholesterol 65mg
Sodium 794mg
Carbohydrate 55g
Dietary Fiber 3g
Sugars 4g
Protein 37g
Dietary Exchanges:
3 starch, 2 vegetable,
3 1/2 lean meat

1 1/2 pounds ground sirloin

1/3 cup plain bread crumbs

3 teaspoons dried oregano leaves, divided

1/4 teaspoon ground cinnamon

1 teaspoon minced garlic

2 tablespoons chopped parsley

2 tablespoons fresh chopped mint, optional

2 egg whites

Salt and pepper to taste

1 (16-ounce) jar marinara sauce

1 (8-ounce) can tomato sauce

2 cups orzo pasta

1/3 cup crumbled reduced-fat feta cheese

Spicy Advice

Orzo is a rice shaped pasta but any pasta may be used.

1. Preheat broiler. Coat baking pan with nonstick cooking spray or line with foil.

2. In bowl, combine meat, bread crumbs, 2 teaspoons oregano, cinnamon, garlic, parsley, mint, egg whites, and season to taste; mixing well. Shape into meatballs (about 18). Place on prepared pan, and broil 5-7 minutes on each side; remove from oven.

3. In large nonstick skillet coated with nonstick cooking spray, heat marinara sauce, tomato sauce, and remaining 1 teaspoon oregano. Add cooked meatballs, cook over medium heat until well heated.

4. Meanwhile, prepare orzo according to package directions. Drain. Serve meatballs and sauce over orzo. Sprinkle with feta cheese, serve.

Great Greek Meatballs with Orzo

Mexican Meatloaf

Nutritional information per serving:

Calories 167
Calories from fat 26%
Fat 5g
Saturated Fat 2g
Cholesterol 47mg
Sodium 533mg
Carbohydrate 11g
Dietary Fiber 1g
Sugars 2g
Protein 20g
Dietary Exchanges:
1 other carbohydrate,
2 1/2 lean meat

The ultimate Sunday comfort food gets a southwestern makeover! Easy to prepare with taco seasoning mix and salsa, this moist meatloaf will become a daily dinner.

Makes 6-8 servings

1/2 cup old-fashioned oatmeal

1 1/4 cups salsa, divided

1 1/2 pounds ground sirloin

1 onion, finely chopped

1 egg white

1 (1.25-ounce) package taco
    seasoning mix

1 (4-ounce) can green chilies

Salt and pepper to taste

1/3 cup reduced-fat shredded Mexican
    blend cheese, optional

1. Preheat oven 350°F. Coat 9x5x3-inch loaf pan with nonstick cooking spray.

2. In large bowl, combine oatmeal and 1 cup salsa. Let sit 5 minutes. Add meat, onion, egg white, taco seasoning mix, and green chilies, mixing well. Season to taste.

3. Transfer meat mixture into prepared pan. Bake 1 hour or until meat is done. Spoon remaining 1/4 cup salsa and cheese, if desired, over top, and continue baking 5 minutes longer. Let stand at least 5 minutes before cutting.

Mexican Meatloaf

Mandarin Steak Stir-Fry

Medium-Dark Roast

Nutritional information per serving:

Calories 273
Calories from fat 28%
Fat 8g
Saturated Fat 2g
Cholesterol 55mg
Sodium 496mg
Carbohydrate 23g
Dietary Fiber 2g
Sugars 17g
Protein 26g
Dietary Exchanges:
1 fruit, 1/2 other carbohydrate,
3 lean meat

Special and speedy, this delectable recipe has it all with a sweet and spicy sauce along with asparagus, peppers, and oranges sprinkled with toasty sesame seeds. Serve over rice, try brown rice. I tested the Orange Marinade in both a salad recipe (page 204) and this stir-fry and couldn't decide which was best, so you now have both options.

Makes 4 servings

1 (16-ounce) sirloin steak (skirt steak or flank steak)
Orange Marinade (see page 204)
1 tablespoon canola oil
1 cup asparagus spears tips
1 cup sliced red bell pepper
1 tablespoon cornstarch

1/4 cup water
3 tablespoons sweet chili sauce
3 tablespoons low-sodium soy sauce
1/4 cup orange juice
1 (11-ounce) can mandarin oranges, drained
1 teaspoon sesame seeds, toasted

1. In resealable plastic bag or shallow dish, add steak to Orange Marinade (recipe page 204) and marinate 2 hours or overnight.

2. Remove steak from marinade and slice. In large nonstick skillet over medium high heat, heat oil and stir-fry steak, asparagus and red pepper, cooking and stirring several minutes.

3. In small bowl, mix together cornstarch and water. Add to skillet with sweet chili sauce, soy sauce, and orange juice, mixing well.

4. Cook until mixture comes to a boil; sauce thickens and meat is done. Add oranges. Sprinkle with sesame seeds, serve over rice.

Pork and Broccoli Stir-Fry

Nutritional information per serving:

Calories 330
Calories from fat 21%
Fat 7g
Saturated Fat 2g
Cholesterol 111mg
Sodium 680mg
Carbohydrate 24g
Dietary Fiber 5g
Sugars 9g
Protein 39g
Dietary Exchanges:
1 starch, 2 vegetable,
4 lean meat

Craving Chinese but don't want to go out? This quick, fantastic family pleaser resulted from pork tenderloin in my fridge and needing dinner pronto.

Makes 4 (1 cup) servings

1 1/2 pounds boneless pork tenderloin, sliced in strips

1/4 cup cornstarch

1 tablespoon sesame oil

1 red bell pepper, cored and cut into strips

2 cups broccoli florets

1 teaspoon minced garlic

1 cup fat-free chicken broth

1 teaspoon grated fresh ginger

1/4 cup hoisin sauce

1 tablespoon seasoned rice vinegar

2 tablespoons low-sodium soy sauce

1/2 cup grated carrots

1 bunch green onions, chopped

Toasted sesame seeds, optional

Serve with rice, try brown rice for added fiber and nutrition.

1. In resealable plastic bag, combine pork strips with cornstarch, coating well.

2. In large nonstick skillet coated with nonstick cooking spray, heat oil over medium high heat and stir-fry pork strips 5-7 minutes. Add bell pepper, broccoli, garlic, broth and ginger, scraping bits from bottom of pan.

3. In small bowl, mix together hoisin sauce, vinegar, and soy sauce; add to pork mixture in skillet. Add carrots and continue cooking until pork is tender. Add green onions. Sprinkle with sesame seeds, if desired. Serve.

Pork and Broccoli Stir-Fry

Garlic Fried Rice

A quick and easy slightly-sweet fragrant rice that's fantastic with spicy foods and sauces.

Makes 6 (1/2 cup) servings

2 cups water
1 cup basmati rice
2 tablespoons olive oil
1 tablespoon minced garlic

1. In medium nonstick pot, bring water and rice to boil, reduce heat, and cover until done (follow package instructions).

2. While rice is cooking, in medium nonstick skillet, heat oil, and cook garlic until starts to turn light brown, watch carefully so doesn't get dark brown. Add cooked rice, serve.

Spicy Advice

Basmati rice is a variety of long grain known for its fragrant flavor and grown in India and Pakistan.

Hoisin Vinaigrette

From a salad to lettuce wraps, this zippy vinaigrette adds zing to whatever you serve it with.

Makes 5 (about 2 tablespoon) servings

2 tablespoons finely chopped red onion
1 teaspoon minced garlic
2 tablespoons hoisin sauce
1/4 cup seasoned rice wine vinegar
1 tablespoon sesame oil
2 tablespoons olive oil
Salt and pepper to taste

1. In small bowl, whisk together all ingredients.

Diva Dermatology

Applelicious Wash

As I rubbed this mixture into my skin, my face felt moisturized and my skin soft.
Let dry few minutes then wash with warm water. Refrigerate leftovers.

1 tablespoon apple juice
2 tablespoons skim milk
1 teaspoon honey

Mix ingredients together. Apply to skin in circular motion 1 minute.
Rinse with warm water.

Nutty Honey Scrub (normal skin)

Oatmeal, almonds and walnuts naturally exfoliate while honey moisturizes creating
the perfect blend scrub to revitalize skin. Refrigerate leftovers.

1/3 cup oatmeal
1-2 tablespoons honey
1 tablespoon apple cider vinegar

1 teaspoon ground almonds
1 teaspoon ground walnuts

Combine all ingredients and apply mixture liberally to moistened face for
10 minutes. Remove with warm washcloth and splash with cool water.

Healthy Honey Mask

Egg is nourishing and honey is moisturizing. Yogurt is loaded with lactic acid, an
ingredient that leaves skin soft and smooth.

1 teaspoon honey
1/4 lemon, juiced

1/2 cup plain yogurt
1 egg white, whipped

In bowl, mix together honey, lemon and yogurt. Stir in egg white. Apply to face 15
minutes. Gently wipe off with damp wash cloth.

Spicy Advice

*For quick moisturizing lift,
apply pure honey to your
skin weekly.*

Cucumber Face Mask (oily skin)

Very exfoliating and cleansing leaving the face smooth, fresh and clean. The cold mixture is so soothing and refreshing. Refrigerate leftovers.

1 small cucumber, peeled and pureed
1/2 cup oatmeal
1 tablespoon plain yogurt

In bowl, make paste by mixing cucumber and oatmeal. Mix one teaspoon of paste with yogurt, leave on face 30 minutes and then rinse.

Avocado Carrot Cream Mask

A really 'good-for-you' mask with vitamin E rich avocados (moisturizer), carrots (high in beta-carotene and antioxidants-reduces dry, flaky skin) and vitamin packed egg — these ingredients will rebuild skin collagen, improve tone and texture, and fade age spots. Leaves you glowing! Makes a lot.

1 avocado, mashed
1 carrot, cooked and mashed
1/2 cup heavy cream

1 egg, beaten
3 tablespoons honey

In bowl, mix all ingredients until smooth. Spread gently over face and neck 10-15 minutes. Rinse with cool water and follow with toner.

Avocado Banana Mask (combination skin)

Bananas contain potassium and vitamins A, B, C and E, which soften, nourish and moisturize leaving your skin feeling smooth.

1/4 ripe banana
1/4 ripe avocado

1 tablespoon plain yogurt
1/2 teaspoon olive oil

Puree all ingredients in blender. Apply to face 15 minutes. Rinse with warm water and pat dry.

Banana Yogurt Nourishing Mask

Went on easy, very cool and soothing — felt very nourishing and moisturizing.

2 tablespoons plain yogurt
1 tablespoon honey
1/4 ripe banana, mashed

In bowl, mix together all ingredients and apply to face and neck for 10 minutes. Rinse with damp wash cloth.

Strawberry and Papaya Mask (combination)

The fruit acids will remove the dead skin and leave a beautiful, hydrated glow. Strawberries are great for skincare due to mildly astringent properties. Oatmeal is calming leaving your face very smooth and buffed. Not for sensitive skin.

2 strawberries
1/4 cup mashed papaya

1 teaspoon honey
1 teaspoon oatmeal

In bowl, combine both fruits together to form thin paste. Add honey and oatmeal to make paste. Apply to face 10 minutes. Rinse.

Berry Tightening Mask

Strawberries contain good source of salicylic acid that removes dead cells and cleans pores. Good for oily skin to improve texture, minimize greasiness and encourage a healthy and more radiant complexion. The folic acid and nutrients have been shown to fight acne.

1/2 teaspoon lemon juice

1 egg white

1 teaspoon honey (heat in microwave for few seconds to thin)

2 strawberries, mashed

In small bowl, blend together all ingredients. Apply to face for 5-10 minutes. Rinse.

Autumn Mask (all skin types)

Skin felt soft and sage had a nice clean smell. Many masks have honey as it also has antibacterial properties, which help calm acne and breakouts, brightening and energizing skin.

1 tablespoon honey

2 tablespoons orange juice

1 apple, pureed

1/2 teaspoon sage

In bowl, mix together honey and orange juice. Add apple puree and sage, mixing well. In microwave-safe bowl, heat mixture 30 seconds or just until warmed. Apply evenly on face 20 minutes. Wash with warm washcloth.

Peach Tightening Mask

As mask dries, it tightens on skin, leaving skin soft and fresh.

1/4 cup mashed peach
1 egg white
1 tablespoon plain yogurt

In blender, combine peach, egg white and yogurt until smooth. Gently pat mixture all over your face for 30 minutes. Rinse with cool water.

Chocolate Mask

Everyone wanted to eat this mask it smelled so good but then it made you look and feel good too! Especially good for dry skin.

1 tablespoon cocoa powder
1 tablespoon heavy cream
1 teaspoon plain yogurt

4 teaspoons honey
1 teaspoon oatmeal

Mix all ingredients in blender and smooth onto face. Leave on for 10 minutes then rinse with warm water.

Pumpkin Mask

Pumpkin (high in vitamins A and C, and zinc) helps remove dead skin, leaving skin feeling nourished and with a nice glow afterwards. Cool smell with relaxing undertones. Refrigerate leftovers.

1/4 cup mashed pumpkin
1 egg
1 tablespoon honey

Whisk together pumpkin, egg and honey. Slather mixture on face 15-20 minutes and rinse.

Margarita Salt Body Buffer

Lime and tequila are natural antiseptics so help detoxify skin and improve tone and texture. Good for hands — felt so soft afterwards.

Makes 1 1/2 cups (1/4 cup per body)

1 cup fine sea salt
2 ounces olive oil

Juice of one lime
3/4 ounces white tequila

In bowl, mix together sea salt, olive oil, lime, and white tequila. In the shower, rub mixture onto damp skin in gentle circular motion. If salt feels too gritty, add more olive oil.

Brown Sugar Scrub

Your hands or whatever body part you scrub felt so soft afterwards. Olive oil contains vitamin E and antioxidants — good for nails.

1/2 cup light brown sugar
1/2 cup olive oil

Mix together and use on hand, feet or body. Rinse.

Strawberry Hand Exfoliate

Margarita Salt Body Buffer

Brown Sugar Scrub

Strawberry Hand Exfoliate

Strawberries contain a natural fruit acid which aids in exfoliation leaving your hands feeling super soft.

8-10 strawberries
2 tablespoons olive oil
1 teaspoon coarse salt, (Kosher or sea salt)

In small bowl, mix together all ingredients. Massage into hands and feet, rinse, and pat dry.

Fruit Smoothie Hair Mask

My hair felt so soft and manageable. I put the other half of the banana, and 1/4 cantaloupe with 1 tablespoon yogurt and had a quick smoothie!

1/2 banana

1/4 avocado

1/4 cantaloupe

1 tablespoon olive oil

1 tablespoon yogurt

In food processor or blender, blend all ingredients. Leave in hair 15 minutes. Rinse.

Coconut Protein Hair Treatment

Protein from eggs and moisturizing qualities of other ingredients revive even the most damaged hair. The fatty acids in eggs make hair shiny and manageable. Use weekly for one month, then monthly.

2 eggs

3 tablespoons coconut milk

2 tablespoons honey

2 tablespoons olive oil

1 tablespoon vanilla extract

Mix all ingredients in bowl with fork until combined. Apply to wet hair prior to shampooing. Leave on 30 minutes. Rinse well with warm water. Shampoo as usual.

Quick Baking Soda Solution

Removes conditioner build-up from hair.

Baking soda

Rub in and rinse thoroughly, then shampoo with your regular products.

Index

ORDER BLANK

Holly Clegg's trim&TERRIFIC® Too Hot In The Kitchen   _____ copies @ $24.95

Holly Clegg's trim&TERRIFIC® Gulf Coast Favorites   _____ copies @ $24.95

The New Holly Clegg trim&TERRIFC® Cookbook   _____ copies @ $29.95

Holly Clegg's trim&TERRIFIC® Home Entertaining   _____ copies @$29.95

Holly Clegg's trim&TERRIFIC® Freezer Friendly Meals   _____ copies @ $19.95

Holly Clegg's trim&TERRIFIC® Diabetic Cooking   _____ copies @ $18.95

Eating Well Through Cancer   _____ copies @ $24.95

SUBTOTAL _____

(Louisiana residents add 8.9%) TAX _____

Postage and Handling ($4.00) _____

Postage and handling for each additional book ($1.00) _____

TOTAL _____

Name _____

Address _____

City_____State_____Zip Code _____

Telephone Number_____Email Address _____

PLEASE CHARGE to my ☐ MasterCard ☐ Visa

Card # _____ Expiration _____

Signature of Cardholder _____

MAIL CHECK TO:
Holly Clegg
13431 Woodmont Court
Baton Rouge, LA 70810
*Make checks payable to
Holly B. Clegg, Inc.*

OR CHARGE BY PHONE
1-800-88HOLLY

VISIT MY WEBSITE:
www.hollyclegg.com or www.thehealthycookingblog.com